MW00954849

Table of Conten.

Table of Contents 1

Copyright Notice 4

About The Author 5

Part 1: So, You Want To Be A Translator 7

Why Become A Translator 8

Freelance Working Conditions 8

Translating Part-Time 10

You're The Boss 10

Money, Money, Money! 10

Do I Need Any Special Skills Or Experience? 12

Types Of Translation Work 13

General Translations 14

Technical Translations 15

Medical Translations 15

Software, Game & Mobile App Localization 16

Subtitle & Voice-Over Translation 18

In-House Translation Jobs vs. Freelancing 20

A Financially Safe Environment 20

Experience Build-Up 21

Free & Continuous Training 22

Business & Social Networking 22

Having It Both Ways 23

Software Tools Of The Trade 23

Do I Need Them? 24

Basic Tools 24

Specialized Tools 25

Part 2: Computer-Assisted Translation (CAT) Tools: A Crash Course 26

So, What's A CAT Tool? 27

A Short Introduction 27

User Interface Overview 29
CAT Tools Panorama! 31
Translation Memories (TMs) **38**
What's a Translation memory? 38
TM Match Categories 39
Word Counts, The Trados Discount Model & Weighted Words **43**
The Trados Discount Model 45
Weighted Words 48
Terminology Databases (TermBases) **50**
Handoff & Delivery Packages **53**
Handoff Packages 53
Delivery Packages 55
A Typical Translation Project Workflow **56**
Client Handoff 56
Translation 59
Proofreading & Spell-Checking 66
Verification Checks 67
Delivery / Handback 69
Machine Translation (MT) **72**
Avoiding CAT Tool Lock-In **74**
Freeing Past & Existing Translations 75
Keeping Your Future Work Cross-Platform 75
CAT Tools On A Mac Or GNU/Linux **76**
Native CAT Tools 77
Virtualized CAT Tools 79

Part 3: Running A Freelance Translation Business **82**
Defining Your Core Language Pairs **83**
Setting Up Your Pricelist **84**
Rates For Translation Agencies 85
Rates For Direct (Non-Agency) Customers 86
Minimum Charge 87
Indicative Word Rate & Minimum Charge Ranges 88
Choosing Your CAT Tool **91**

Marketing Your Business (Or How To Find Clients).....93
Creating Or Spicing Up Your Resume/CV 93
Membership-based Translators' Websites 97
Social Networks: LinkedIn, Facebook, Twitter, Google+
....99
Online Business Directories 101
Your Personal Website.................................104
Pro Bono Service...105
Organizing Your Work...**106**
Project Dashboard 106
Tree Folder Structure 110
A Word About Purchase Orders & Invoices 113
Backups! Backups! Backups!.................................114
Client Relationship Quick Tips.................................**118**
Avoiding Fraudulent Clients **122**

Appendix 1: Translation Industry Glossary **124**

Appendix 2: ISO Language Codes.................**135**

Appendix 3: List of Translation Companies.......**141**

Copyright Notice

About The Author

Author's Photo

I'm an American expat (born and raised in Lynn, Massachu-setts) residing the last two or so decades in Athens, Greece. My professional career revolves around the Translation & Lo-calization Industry for more than 17 years. I started out as a young inexperienced translator and, after years of hard work and persistence, ended up with my last in-house position be-ing that of Translation & Software Localization Director.

Translation and software localization are my core specialties, having translated or project managed numerous projects for Microsoft, IBM/Lotus, Adobe, Symantec, GE Energy, Cater-pillar, Toshiba, LaCie, Canon, Sony, Nokia, Bosch, Siemens, just to mention a few.

Lately, I'm freelancing and providing translation & localiza-tion consulting to companies within the industry (i.e., trans-lation agencies), and to corporations in need of internal or ex-ternal translation/localization services (i.e., international firms with overseas branch offices, software companies and so on).

I'm also actively involved in helping out translators/localizers, especially with their translation software tools and daily business operation. A considerable effort in this area is pro bono. Seeing a lack of an online solution to such issues, I've set up a website to deal with them: http://www.translators-tech-help.com.

Petro Dudi

July 29th, 2015

Argyroupoli, Attika, Greece

Part 1: So, You Want To Be A Translator...

In this introductory part we'll cover topics that are of interest to anyone contemplating on getting involved with translations, or to existing translators that are just starting out. We'll delve into freelance working conditions, check whether any skills or experience is required, look at the types of translation work and tools available, and compare translation freelancing to in-house translation positions.

Why Become A Translator

Since you're reading these lines, you've pretty much set your mind on becoming a translator (or you might be one already, and wish to enrich your knowledge even further). Moreover, I assume you're at least bilingual (speak and write in two languages), as this is the only real prerequisite you'll be needing here for starting out as a translator.

Your decision to invest time and money to learn more about the craft is quite wise. Despite what you've heard or read, doing translations isn't a simple walk in the park. There are rules to be followed, special tools to be used, and particular ways of running a freelance translation business. But, you've chosen one of the best guides out there to teach you all these and more in the most comprehensive, easy to follow way.

So, why should you become a translator? If we tackle it from the most obvious angle, the career perspective, you'll find a host of interesting benefits that are hardly ever found in other job descriptions. And what are these, you might wonder? Well, for the most important ones, we have the following:

Freelance Working Conditions

The dream of every cubicle-confined employee can become a reality for you.

Work From Anywhere

Bye-bye commuting. Welcome **tele**-commuting.

Be the envy of the cubicle tribe when you sit each day in front of your computer to work.

—

In your comfy home.

In your cozy pajamas.

Your cat next to you. *Purring.*

You get the picture. Tired of sitting inside all day (or can't stand that purring anymore)? Why not continue your translation work from your favorite coffee shop? It's an option, too. Actually, it's one of the hundreds of options you have. So, take advantage of it.

Set Your Own Working Hours

Not a 9-to-5 type of person? No problem. Pick your favorite hours during the day (or night) and start translating. You can even split up the time in any suitable (or crazy) scheme you can imagine. Maybe the graveyard shift works better for you. You just never know and might even be surprised with your output during specific hours.

Define Your Price

For once, you have the power to set your price. But, with great power comes great responsibility. If you overdo it with your rates then you will have the exact opposite effect: lower earnings. I will explain in **Part 3 - Running A Freelance Translation Business** how to properly set up your price list, so for now just keep in mind that you have the privilege of establishing your own prices.

Translating Part-Time

Being a freelancer doesn't always mean you are a full-time freelancer as well. Maybe you already have a day job and would just like to translate for that extra income. Or, it could be the case that you have another part-time job too, so you would like to take advantage of your free time and translate so you can have a reasonable total income per month.

Whatever your situation is, know that you can treat your freelance translation job as another part-time stint if necessary.

You're The Boss

Although this one kind of incorporates all the previous points, it still deserves its own space. For maybe the first time in your whole professional life, you're the *boss*. Well, okay, you're not the typical boss (having an army of employees to harass whenever you feel like), but at least you're the CEO of Me Myself & I Inc. Your decisions and management style affect your company's bottom line (a.k.a. your own pocket). You're also responsible for the viability, that is the life-span, of your endeavor. Pretty important stuff, right? But don't worry. As long as you function normally and stick to the advice in this guide (and apply some common sense), you should be fine.

Money, Money, Money!

Well, duh!

You're obviously looking into this professional career path because you wish to increase (or create from scratch) your fortunes (unless you're a hardcore hobbyist translator in which case money is anathema; if you're such a person contact me as I've always wanted to meet one).

The amount of money and how quickly you make it will depend on a series of parameters such as:

- Language pair(s) you handle (some languages fare better)
- Translation rates (including minimum charges)
- Daily output (words or pages)
- Availability (weekdays, weekends, holidays)
- Business visibility (can clients find you easily?)

The above parameters also control the steadiness of your business. By this I mean the frequency in which you receive work. The shorter the gap between projects, the better in terms of earnings. This is a crucial part of the job, and if it's dysfunctional you're financial planning goes down a random, what-now trail that will make your life a bit more complicated.

As mentioned further above, if you're a sensible enough individual and read this whole guide carefully (and consult it now-and-then during your business activity), you'll be all right. I'll show you how to properly set things up and start taking in steady work that will guarantee a good stream of revenue. Translating for a living can generate surprising amounts of money and, often enough, you'll be doing this with minimum effort too.

Do I Need Any Special Skills Or Experience?

Going against the common belief here, the short answer is no. You don't need any prior experience or any special skill, other than knowing apparently how to speak and write in a second language. Before you start wondering whether I'm pulling your leg, I strongly urge you to keep reading to see how this is possible. Normally, wouldn't you need some knowledge of the terminology of specific subject fields, or at the very least, have some sort of prior background experience in those industries? Let me explain here why this isn't strictly so.

If you're a beginner in the translation business, you would assume you don't have any experience in any translation field. Common sense implies that you need a lot of time and related translation projects to start gaining experience in a number of those. But, no one is forcing you to start working on projects that aren't in your domain of interest and knowledge. And you actually do have some knowledge of specific domains even without knowing it upfront.

If you think about it carefully, even as a newcomer to this trade you already possess a range of special knowledge in the form of prior, unrelated work activities, hobbies and general interests. For example, a person's last job could've been in the Human Resources (HR) Department of a company. This person's job responsibilities could've included recruitment handling, working guidelines, payment management, external vendor coordination, etc. Now let's say this person gets involved in translating a project regarding HR material. Wouldn't he/she be able to handle the project and use the proper terminology and lingo? I strongly believe he/she would've done a great translation.

Another example: You're a hardcore video game player, spending many of your free hours in front of your game console, your PC or Mac, or even your tablet/smart phone. You possibly play a list of different genre games, like MMORPGs (Massively Multiplayer Online Role-Playing Games), FPSs (First-Person Shooters), Strategy and Puzzle video games. Wouldn't it be feasible for you to translate a project that related to any of these game genres? And doing it in the most professional and accurate way? I don't see why this couldn't work. You already know the terminology and lingo of the games, so you're the best option for such translation work.

I think you get where this is going regarding having prior skills for becoming a translator. In short, we all have such skills and knowledge but simply need to dig deep down and pull them out into the open. Once you put this precious knowledge in order, you've set the basis on seeking and handling any relevant translation project.

Types Of Translation Work

The translation industry has reached a critical mass lately, especially these last two decades, and is moving forward even stronger. The driving force behind this push is globalization. Our world has become smaller and smaller in terms of communications, product availability and traveling just to name a few.

Companies aren't restricted anymore to their own city, country or even continent. Nowadays, they can offer their products and services world-wide, in any language and continent. This creates an urgent universal need for translation and localization services in nearly all languages spoken on this planet. And, due to the diversity of the content being exchanged globally, these translation and localization services are required in diverse subject fields such as company business correspondence, corporate websites, technical manuals, marketing material, medical devices, TV & movie scripts, software, etc.

Here, I'm going to outline the most common types of translation work that clients (i.e., translation agencies or non-agencies like direct customers) request. This way you'll get a quick overview of what you'll be dealing with.

General Translations

Starting with the easiest of all, this category contains all those topics that are trivial to deal with and have no technical difficulty whatsoever. Such subjects could be: agreements, email correspondence, leaflets, forms, charters, notes, warranties, contracts, guarantees, notices, pro formas, etc.

You shouldn't experience any problems with this translation type. Furthermore, you'll quickly find out that these subjects will allow you to handle larger volumes and in astonishingly shorter completion times.

Technical Translations

This kind of translation work is more demanding and, quite possibly, you'll be encountering requests for it more frequently than any other of the types outlined here. The tech domain of course includes vast subcategories, but we can classify them in major groups such as: electronics, engineering, automotive, aviation, military, etc.

You'll usually be dealing with user or maintenance/parts manuals, technical specification sheets, Quality Assurance (QA) reports and the likes.

Don't freak out if you don't have a clue about some or nearly all of these tech fields. You'll never be required to know all of them, and to be frank, there's no way you can master the whole bunch. You should stick to those few you understand best, and to the ones you're willing to learn more about.

Medical Translations

Another quite challenging type of translation work is the medical field. And, like the technical field described above, it can be categorized into sub-groups such as: life sciences, medical devices, biomedicine, dentistry, neurology, toxicology, genetics, etc.

Evidently, you must have some background experience to be able to tackle medical translation projects. The client's requiring such work will most likely request proof of your medical experience and knowledge. So, you'll either start working on these if you already have any suitable medical background (i.e., you're a doctor, therapist, or medical field graduate, etc.), or learn and deal with the very basic, thus easier, medical types such as life sciences.

As a side note, medical translations are considered very good paying projects, so in a sense it's worth investing time and effort in mastering a few of its subdomains.

Software, Game & Mobile App Localization

This one is a very interesting field. From our standard desktop and laptop computers to game consoles and mobile devices, the software running on them is a great source for translation material. A vast majority of translation projects revolve around software and mobile apps. But, let me clarify first why we describe the process as **localization** and not simply translation.

Localization as a service (as opposed to translation), usually contains the following processes:

1. Detection and extraction (exporting) of translatable material (i.e., text, audio/video, graphics etc.) from the User Interface (UI) and User Assistance (UA; the help files accompanying the software) elements.
2. Translation of the extracted material (special attention is given to cultural and regional requirements of the target language).
3. Dialog resizing (of windows, buttons, tabs etc.) and string adjustments (due to truncation) in the User Interface (UI).
4. Insertion (importing) of translated material.
5. Functional testing of the software (a.k.a. Software Localization Testing).

The person involved in the above process is called a Software (SW) Localizer (or Software Localization Tester when dealing only with the functioning testing, point 5 above, of the software). To be precise, a SW Localizer mainly deals with points 2 and 3, since the exporting and importing of the material is handled by the SW Localization Tool.

So, if we are to oversimplify the distinction between a typical translator and a SW Localizer, we'd say that a SW Localizer is burdened with an additional task of adjusting the layout of the windows, buttons, tabs and text that appear on a device's screen (a.k.a. User Interface). The truth is that lately even this process of UI resizing has been automated quite a lot with advanced SW Localization Tools, thus leaving to the SW Localizer the need to just confirm the changes. The same is true for Software Localization Testing; new and advanced automated SW Localization Testing Suites allow for rigid functional testing of any software, reducing the SW Localization Tester's duties to that of a mere observer.

Now that you know the difference between a translator and a localizer, let me add that, lately, there seems to be a decline in projects that request freelance localization services. It seems that this service is mostly handled in-house nowadays, meaning that you'll most probably find such a position available internally, within a company rather than as a pure freelance option. This isn't necessarily bad, as you could arrange a contract and work internally until the localization project is over. After that, you're free to either continue your freelancing translation work or extend the in-house contract. Plus, you can have it both ways, and combine your in-house company work along with your freelancing stint, unless circumstances don't permit it.

Moreover, in recent years it's become a trend for clients (translation agencies or direct software houses) to request the translation of software strings only (UI text) with no hint of the other localization chores. And usually, these strings are provided in tabular form (i.e., spreadsheets), with character length limitations and screenshots displaying the actual text in context. This makes the process a more regular translation job, but special attention is needed with the character length limits.

Subtitle & Voice-Over Translation

Two other popular translation types are subtitle and voice-over translations. Generally, the subject fields are easier here since the content is mostly from TV series, documentaries, movies, etc. These two are also distinguished by the fact that, most often, they are assigned by Film/TV Studios and thus, in a lesser extent by translation agencies. Furthermore, the pricing model is usually different from the regular per word or per page charge we see in the industry. So here, the common payment option offered for these services is per episode, or per series (a series is usually a group of 12 or 24 episodes). Below, I'll outline what these two translation services are all about.

Subtitle Translation

Subtitles for translation are always provided in a file that contains the lines of text and their time-codes. The time-codes tell the device playing the video when to pop-up each line thus keeping everything nice and synced. Your job would always be to touch the text parts and never fiddle with the time-codes. Also, you should know that your restrictions when translating subtitles include the following:

1. Each line of text shouldn't be over 45-50 characters in length
2. Each time-code should contain a maximum of 2 lines

So, if your target language has the tendency of inflating the text (unfortunately, most of the languages out there do this), then you'll have to start cutting corners and tighten your translations to the above requirements. A positive side here is that you can use specialized subtitling software that make sure to notify and assist you when reaching (or exceeding) any subtitling requirements.

Voice-Over Translations

No, you won't be doing the actual voice-over, although there is a market for that too, but that topic isn't within the reach of this guide. What happens in this type of translation service, is that you're provided with the same script the original actors used in the production of the TV episodes or movie. Sometimes, this script will contain director instructions (camera angles, scenery description, etc.) which are usually in caps and are placed before each actual dialogue. You usually ignore these instructions and don't need to translate them, unless instructed to do otherwise.

Your task is to translate the dialogues, but as with everything in this world, there's catch. When you start translating, you're required to keep the same time duration for each one of them, compared to the original language. This is very important otherwise the customer (Film/TV Studio or translation agency) won't be able to lip-sync correctly your translations. However, unlike subtitling material, there are no time-codes in a voice-over script which keep you on track. So, how are you going to pull this off? Well, based on years of personally translating voice-over scripts, I can suggest the following great tip:

Once you translate a dialogue, read aloud again the source version and time in your head the duration you need to say it. Do the same thing for the target version. For a correct lip-synced translation you need both time durations to match. Once you get the hang of it, you'll start doing it unconsciously and without the need to read it aloud.

It's also worth mentioning here that some clients could request you to insert breaks into the translated voice-over script. These breaks are pauses in the spoken dialogue, and could be either short or long in duration. Usually, the symbol used to report these breaks is the slash character ("/"). A single slash means a short break and a double slash ("//") denotes a long one. And, I'm afraid, the only way to know whether there is any type of break in the dialogue is by watching the video.

In-House Translation Jobs vs. Freelancing

This topic can be tackled from so many sides that a whole guide could be devoted to it. For this reason, I'll be focusing on aspects that are not usually highlighted by other sources, and mainly be describing the benefits and drawbacks of an in-house job, since we covered the freelance aspect further above, in section **Freelance Working Conditions**.

A Financially Safe Environment

It's quite clear that we're all living in an erratic and fluid financial world, never knowing when the next big crisis will hit us straight in the face. That's one of the reasons companies, with their own internal mini-world of politics, finances and business procedures, strive to shield themselves from the negative impacts of the outer, real world. The better they accomplish this, the more successful they are as a business.

So, evidently, companies should be a great place to work at when looking at it from the financial safety side of things. A fixed salary can guarantee less anxiety in your life and allow you to focus on other important things. This is quite crucial, since a freelancer has to plan ahead and make sure he/she has a constant stream of work to sustain any financial viability.

Experience Build-Up

Another good thing about company ecosystems is that they allow you to expand and sharpen your skills. The longer you stay with a company, the more experience you'll acquire and this is invaluable, believe me. Nowhere else will you be able to witness nearly all the types of translation work and processes (assuming here that you're working for a translation company). It's the best hands-on experience you'll ever find. All the knowledge you'll gain from an in-house job position can, and should, be used as your foundation for any freelancing career you might seek afterwards. In fact, the majority of professional freelance translators started out exactly this way!

Free & Continuous Training

A nice added bonus to an in-house job is the free and ongoing training you receive from your company department. They'll make sure to keep you up to date with all the latest tools and procedures and show you how to maximize their utilization within the department's workflow. Most likely, you'll also acquire certifications from these training courses which can help you considerably with future promotions, or when you go full-time freelancing. Make sure to seek out and take advantage of any such training programs if you land an in-house job. You'll save some money in the long run (these courses cost something, you know) and will be a valuable asset when freelancing.

Business & Social Networking

Don't ever underestimate the power of networking. Within a company environment you can connect each day with a myriad of people (colleagues, managers, vendors, customers, etc.) who could prove extremely useful sooner or later in your in-house career or freelancing attempt. Try keeping contact with them as much as possible, keep their contact details handy, and never forget to remind them that you're always around if they need any help. This behavior, which is a mix of business networking and social engineering, will keep you on their A-list. So, when you come around asking for their help, chances are, they'll be more than happy to give it.

And, as you might have guessed, when you decide to go freelancing these contacts will prove to be a gold mine. They will open important doors in your path allowing you to increase your freelance business.

Of course, it's not all blissful when working internally for a company. Most likely, you'll be confined to a cubicle or a small office space. You'll be forced to follow fixed, inflexible working hours, and have some peculiar Pointy-Haired Boss (PHB) on your back. Plus, there's always the probability of having limited career options when you're down this path.

Having It Both Ways

But wait! You could still have the best of both worlds. In today's versatile corporate working environments there are companies that allow, and even prefer, putting on their payroll freelancers. As a freelancer under contract you can work in-house for a specific time period (usually during a project's life-cycle) and harvest the benefits offered by such positions. So don't rule out such job vacancies.

Software Tools Of The Trade

As with every profession, there are tools of the trade that make your life a lot easier when dealing with your everyday work. And, as it is with all tools, there are basic and specialized versions of them depending on the complexity of your task. I'll give you a brief overview here since we'll delve into them thoroughly in the next part, **Part 2: Computer-Assisted Translation (CAT) Tools: A Crash Course.**

Do I Need Them?

Well... yes. You do need them. In either the basic or specialized tool form, your working life will be much easier than without them. And depending on your domain of expertise or field inclination, it would be a matter of having any business or not.

Basic Tools

Since we're well into the computer era, all translations are conducted on some type of computer system. So it's quite reasonable to state here that you need at least a basic software tool to translate (unless you're so old-school you still use that typewriter of yours). The most simple form of such a tool is the word processor software. In these days we have a plethora of them, ranging from the free OpenOffice/LibreOffice Writer, to paid ones such as Microsoft Word or Apple's Pages. Depending on your translation project's requirements, you could get away with using only a word processor, but could face a lower stream of work if you only allow this tool in your workflow.

Specialized Tools

Specialized translation tools are called CAT Tools in our industry and, no, they don't have anything to do with those cute felines. The initials stand for Computer-Assisted Translation, and they do exactly that. These tools offer methods for quicker and larger translation turn-overs, better quality and consistent terminology handling, just to name a few. Once you get used to them (and you'll get the gist of them in the next part of this guide), you'll be wondering how on earth you lived without them.

Let me make clear here that CAT Tools have nothing to do with Machine Translation (MT). Machine Translation tools (such as Google Translate, Babylon, etc.) are automated, pure software based translations with no human involvement. Thus, the results are quite funny, to say the least (although the technology is reaching a point where the results are getting better and better, but still not close to a human-based translation). CAT Tools require from an actual human translator to do the work but make the process a lot easier. And, as if this wasn't weird enough, CAT Tools have the ability to interface with Machine Translation platforms, and pull in those awkward translations. The logic behind this interfacing is that the translator can then review the MT translations and adapt them to his/her needs with less effort and time (in most cases, though, and depending on subject field, the effort could be quite larger and the translator might be better off translating from scratch those parts).

Part 2: Computer-Assisted Translation (CAT) Tools: A Crash Course

In this part of the guide we'll get down to details regarding the tools a translator uses every day. My aim here is to provide you with information not only from the translator's perspective but also from the viewpoint of the translation engineer and translation project manager. This will allow you to gain valuable insight into how industry professionals use these tools. I won't burden you with irrelevant facts or academic knowledge of CAT Tools (there's enough of that in the tools' manuals). Instead, we'll focus on a hands-on approach, and on how you can take advantage of them regardless of your CAT Tool of choice.

So, What's A CAT Tool?

A Short Introduction

Computer-Assisted Translation Tools, or CAT Tools, are specialized computer programs that, as the name implies, aid the translator during translation activities. Nowadays, they're available in suites rather than separate programs that communicate with each other, so you could think of them as a kind of integrated translation environment. We'll get a better glimpse of the user interface in the following section, **User Interface Overview**.

A CAT Tool's first and foremost function is the successful extraction of all translatable content from a source file. A source file could be anything from an MS Word document, an Excel Spreadsheet, a PowerPoint presentation, an InDesign file, an HTML file, or any other supported file format. The extracted material is then available through the CAT Tool's Editor pane, in tabular form that's easy on the eyes and allows for quicker translation processing. Another benefit of the tabular form view a CAT Tool offers is that you only have to focus on the translatable content without having distractions such as images, funny font colors/sizes, or weird backgrounds which you'd regular deal with when translating directly in source files (for example, a PowerPoint file). As an added bonus, you can translate any supported source file even if you don't have the original software that produced it! CAT Tools contain internal parsers that handle these source files and, once translated, can export everything back to the same format.

The next significant feature we have is the retention and re-use of translations. By using a technology called Translation Memories (TMs), all translations are saved in a database for future reference and use. You can think of this process as a kind of translation recycling. What this practically means is that the next time you translate a similar document, the CAT Tool will automatically insert into your work identical translations it finds in the database. Moreover, it will also suggest possible translations on near-identical text parts, so you can then simply adjust the similar translation to the exact context of the new one. This is a vital tool in your hands, as it will immensely speed up your work and keep it consistent. We'll cover this feature in more detail in section **Translation Memories (TMs)**.

Along with Translation Memories, another nifty feature (and the darling of technical translation projects) is terminology consistency. This is offered through another technology called Terminology Databases (TermBases). The functionality is quite similar to Translation Memories, with the main difference being that TermBases accumulate specific, predefined keywords/phrases (a.k.a. terms). In conjunction with a Translation Memory, the moment you enter a text part that contains a TermBase match, you'll see that term highlighted (in both the text part and the TM pane) and the predefined translation of it shown to you. This way you get a clear indication of what part is an actual term and how to correctly translate it. We'll say more about this in section **Terminology Databases (TermBases)**.

Before we move on and get into details, it's worth mentioning here that CAT Tools also provide you with something called Verification Checks. Unfortunately, a lot of translators underestimate the power and usefulness of this feature. But, in many cases it can prove a life-saver. What these checks do is make sure your translation (completed or in progress) complies with your project's settings. In brief, your work is checked for: untranslated parts, errors within translated parts, character length limits (if enabled by client), inconsistent translations, spelling/grammar errors, and so on. The majority of clients request you run a Verification Check before delivering your work. And, to be honest, you should do it even when not requested. The process will surely catch problems you never knew were there and save your from some possible embarrassing moments with the client.

User Interface Overview

Before we see a real CAT Tool User Interface, let's simplify it by showing the following mockup:

Project/File Pane	Translation Memory	TermBase
	Editor	

CAT Tool User Interface Mockup

This is a quite common layout used by nearly all major CAT Tools. You can see now why we called it an Integrated Translation Environment. In a single screen, you have access to all four major CAT Tool features:

1. Project/File Pane: For handling project/file details
2. Translation Memory: For re-using of previous translations
3. TermBase: For terminology re-use and consistency
4. Editor: For translating

We briefly mentioned earlier most of the above, and we'll review them in detail later on.

Now let's see what an actual CAT Tool screen looks like:

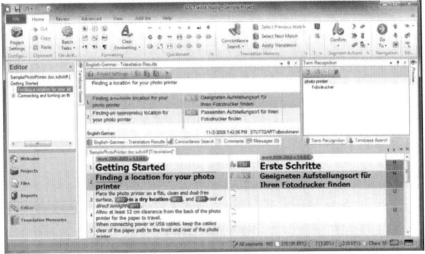

SDL Trados Studio 2014 User Interface

The above screenshot is from SDL Trados Studio 2014. It's one of the most popular proprietary CAT Tools in the industry. Despite the seemingly more complex appearance, the main layout and design follows the simplified mockup we saw further above.

CAT Tools Panorama!

It's true that there's an abundance of CAT Tools in the translation industry, and we're even seeing the first attempts at pure online (cloud) CAT Tools. Just so you know, it wasn't like this a decade or so ago. Back then, you only had a handful of software choices to go with and the price tag was quite forbidding for most translators. Now, we have a lot more proprietary CAT Tools which are cheaper and more capable than ever. Likewise, our geeky friends in the Open Source scene by scratching another itch, have produced some amazing free CAT Tools as well!

I'll introduce to you what I feel are the five most important ones, as of this writing. I'm not a fanboy of any of these, but have used them interchangeably depending on project requirements, since each one handles a bit better specific requirements. So, please don't start a flamewar if you don't see your favorite CAT Tool mentioned here! I'll list them by current industry traction and finish with the free and open source versions.

SDL Trados Studio

License: Proprietary
Company: SDL
Product Website:
http://www.sdl.com/cxc/language/translation-productivity/trados-studio/

Even before being acquired by SDL, Trados Workbench (as was its original product name) was one of the first real CAT Tools in the Translation Industry. Back then each component was a separate program, so you had three programs open at the same time (editor, translation memory, termbase), and these interfaced with each other. When SDL added Trados Workbench to their portfolio, they kept it as is for a couple of releases, and then decided it was best to blend the components into one nice piece of software, hence the creation of the Trados Studio series.

SDL also created SDL OpenExchange, which is a kind of app/plugin-in online store for Trados Studio. You can find many free plug-ins too, which will enhance your work with this CAT Tool.

SDL Trados Studio is one of the most frequently used platforms in the industry, so you can't go wrong investing your money and time on it.

Pros:

- Used widely in the industry
- Covers all major source formats
- Easy task & delivery management (i.e., project and return packages)
- Backwards compatibility with older Trados versions
- Coherent User Interface
- SDL OpenExchange Store

Cons:

- A bit pricy
- Can become sluggish when working on very large files
- TermBase management not included (need to buy SDL MultiTerm)
- Only runs on Microsoft Windows Operating Systems

Wordfast

License: Proprietary
Company: Wordfast
Product Website: http://www.wordfast.com

Wordfast is another popular software, having its roots from the early days of CAT Tools. Back then it was usually the only cheap alternative to Trados Workbench, although with fairly less capabilities (it was actually an MS Word plug-in!), hence the lower price tag. Today, Wordfast is a full-fledged CAT Tool, with its own integrated environment and a host of nice features, and still manages to keep the price low.

What I like in this tool is the clean User Interface, and the clear distinction it offers between the editor and the task management environment. In Wordfast lingo, these are called perspectives, so we have the "TXML editor perspective" and the "PM perspective". Each one is nicely outlined and easy to understand. Plus, this is the only proprietary CAT Tool that runs on all three major operating systems: OS X, MS Windows, and GNU/Linux!

If you're on a budget, make sure to check out this CAT Tool. If it fits your business requirements, it will prove to be a trusty partner in your translation work.

Pros:

- Good price tag
- Popular in the translation industry
- Includes TermBase management
- Straightforward User Interface
- Runs on multiple Operating Systems (OS X, MS Windows, GNU/Linux)

Cons:

- A bit limited in supported source formats

memoQ

License: Proprietary
Company: Kilgray
Product Website: https://www.memoq.com

Once the underdog of the CAT Tools scene, memoQ has made its way up and become a true competitor in the translation tools business. As a newer member, it had to initially focus on being compatible with the competition to be able to lure those users in. And, as a consequence, memoQ is a kind of Swiss army knife, since it can handle all the native formats of other tools (i.e., Trados Studio, Wordfast, etc.) and cope with the myriads of source file formats (i.e., MS Word documents, MS Excel spreadsheets, MS PowerPoint presentations, HTML, etc.).

Furthermore, memoQ offers features unique to its environment which you won't find in any other CAT Tool. These include special Translation Memory handling, clever material referencing, multiple filtering views of your translation content, notable Quality and Verification Checks, and more.

If you're on a budget and need maximum compatibility with top leading CAT Tools, then this is your software. And with the reasonable price tag you get a tool that's ahead of its competition in many serious ways.

Pros:

- Price range
- Handles all major CAT Tool native formats
- Supports numerous source file formats
- Offers features not found in other tools

Cons:

- User Interface is a bit sluggish sometimes

Heartsome Translation Studio

License: Open Source (GPL v2.0)
Company: N/A
Product Website:
https://github.com/heartsome/translationstudio8

This CAT Tool has the most interesting history of all tools mentioned here. It started out as proprietary software by a company named Heartsome (now defunct). The marketing concept for this product was smart, since Heartsome was promoting it as a cheap alternative to the CAT Tools heavyweights. They even managed to create this tool in such a way that it resembled in appearance (but not in functionality) the leading player in the field: Trados Studio. But, they couldn't gain market momentum even when placed that low in the price range. Their last attempt (and hope) was with the latest release which was Heartsome Translation Studio 8. They did their best and incorporated features that were missing, but also introduced some original ideas for the CAT Tool scene. However, luck had run out for Heartsome. They had to close shop.

Here comes the interesting part. Whereas any other company would've either sold their assets (in this case software) or bury them into oblivion, Heartsome decided to go Open Source. This meant changing the software license from proprietary to a free one, allowing anyone to download and use their CAT Tool. Even better, this open source license (GPL v2.0) allowed for the free distribution of the actual source code, so any software developer could start tinkering with it and produce enhanced versions of the tool. The only similar high profile case of proprietary software going Open Source that comes to mind is that of the Netscape web browser, which eventually ended up as today's Firefox.

So, what does this tool have to offer in its latest incarnation? It boasts a new User Interface which aligns it more closely to what you expect from a modern CAT Tool environment, it supports a good set of source and CAT Tool file formats, has nice drag-and-drop project management features, and includes some powerful plug-ins for handling Translation Memories, TermBases, etc.

In short, if you're cash-strapped or just want to get a feeling of an actual CAT Tool suite, Heartsome Translation Studio is the tool for you. Oh, did I mention that it also supports all major Operating Systems (OS X, MS Windows, GNU/Linux)?

Pros:

- It's free!
- Handles most major CAT Tool native formats
- Supports most major source file formats
- Includes Translation Memory & TermBase management
- Runs on multiple Operating Systems (OS X, MS Windows, GNU/Linux)

Cons:

- Can act a bit sluggish on some activities (i.e. File analysis)

OmegaT

License: Open Source (GPL v3.0)
Company: N/A
Product Website: http://www.omegat.org

This is a pure child of the Open Source effort. Way before Heartsome decided to go Open Source, there was no real free and Open Source CAT Tool around. So, there was an itch which needed immediate attention. The resulting software was named OmegaT, and it keeps moving along just fine with refinements and new functionality on each major release.

Compared to the previous CAT Tools mentioned further above, OmegaT may seem succinct in terms of User Interface and features. It doesn't offer the luxuries and eye-candy usually found in other tools; instead, it follows a spartan way of doing things, both visually and functionally. At first, this may scare away a novice user, but if you familiarize yourself with the environment and read the included User Manual, you'll quickly become accustomed to its ways.

OmegaT provides all the basic features you'd expect from such tools, including Translation Memory and Terminology Management, Verification Checks and so on. You could say that the translation editor pane feels a bit old-school and dated, but it serves its job nonetheless. As for file formats support, OmegaT has increased their number lately but still needs to push the envelope here, and make the importing process more straightforward.

Overall, if you'd like to try a CAT Tool that's free, adheres to the purest form of Open Source philosophy and don't mind its few shortcomings, then this is the one to check.

Pros:

- It's free!
- Handles some major CAT Tool native formats
- Supports most major source file formats
- Includes Translation Memory & TermBase management
- Runs on multiple Operating Systems (OS X, MS Windows, GNU/Linux)

Cons:

- Limited functionality compared to major (but non-free) CAT Tools
- Limited CAT Tool file format support
- No batch task management

Translation Memories (TMs)

What's a Translation memory?

As we briefly mentioned earlier in this guide, a Translation Memory is a key component of a CAT Tool. Its core role is to retain all translations that are being created at any given time during the translation process. Furthermore, its other important duty is to present to you either an identical or a similar translation match during the translation phase of a file's segments (a segment is part of a paragraph, a sentence that's defined by a punctuation mark). This last feature is basically a kind of re-cycling of existing translations, a feature which considerably speeds-up the whole process and greatly lowers the overall costs for your client.

We should make clear here that in order for a Translation Memory to provide you with any type of match (identical or similar), it first needs to contain some translations. This sounds obvious, but I've encountered cases where translators were confused because their empty TM wasn't providing any translation matches! So keep this in mind.

Now that we know what a Translation Memory is, we should explore in more detail the translation matches that are presented by a TM.

TM Match Categories

Till now we referred to a TM's translation matches being identical or similar in nature. I've used these simple terms to make it clearer to people not involved yet with CAT Tools. You should also know that TM matches are measured by percentage of match. Thus, the time has come to introduce the actual names and categories these matches have, and what their percentage rate is for each of them.

Note: As we'll see in **Word Counts, The Trados Discount Model & Weighted Words**, another reason for these match categories and their percentage rates is related to the way you get paid for them. This is only relevant when a client requests to apply a TM Match Discount Model (a.k.a. The Trados Discount Model). More on this in the relevant section, as stated above.

Repetitions

As the name denotes, Repetitions are identical, untranslated segments that repeat themselves in a file or document. It's crucial to understand here that we're talking about untranslated segments, when dealing with Repetitions (as opposed to 100% Matches that we'll describe next, and which are identical, translated segments). This means that Repetitions are not part of a TM (so they don't have a percentage match rate either), as only translated segments reside within a Translation Memory.

Also worth mentioning here is that, lately, CAT Tools have introduced the related match category of Cross-File Repetitions. The theory is the same, but extends to multiple files in the project. This category allows for a better understanding of the volume of work when dealing with more than one file.

100% Matches

This match category concerns identical translation matches that reside in a TM, hence the 100% match rate. So, we're dealing with actual translated segments that already exist in a TM. Furthermore, these existing 100% Matches in the TM could have two possible sources of origin:

1. They could've been in there from older project translations.
2. They could've been introduced by a translated Repetition in the current project.

Let me clarify point 2 above. As was said, Repetitions are identical but untranslated segments. So what happens when you translate one of those Repetitions? Well, it becomes an identical but translated segment. Does that ring any bells? Of course it does, since identical, translated segments fall into the 100% Match category. Thus, automatically, you've created a 100% Match segment for those Repetitions in your TM. This means that all the remaining Repetitions for that segment will be converted instantly into 100% Matches! So having lots of Repetitions in a project is a good thing for you (less work)!

Context / Perfect / ICE / 101% Matches

Don't get baffled by the title. They all have the same meaning, and we have to thank the CAT Tool software companies for describing the same thing in so many different ways (good job guys). I'll just pick the Context Match name to keep things simple.

So what's so special about Context Matches? None other than being a better type of 100% Match. This is possible due to the way these matches are defined: a Context Match occurs when there is at least a 100% Match in the TM and the preceding segment is identical in both the TM and document. I know it may seem a bit complicated to grasp, but let me provide you with an example:

100% Match

Origin	Segments
Document	[ABC] [DEF]
Translation Memory	[XYZ] [DEF]

In the above example, segment [DEF] has a different preceding segment in the document ([ABC]) and the TM ([XYZ]). So this makes it a regular 100% Match.

Context Match

Origin	Segments
Document	[ABC] [DEF]
Translation Memory	[ABC] [DEF]

In this example, the preceding segments are identical in both document and TM, so it falls into the definition of a Context Match.

Note that the preceding segment in a TM isn't visible to the user, but that information is stored in there for various uses, one being the calculation of Context Matches.

Fuzzy Matches

The name is unrelated to anything fluffy, despite the fact that we're talking about **CAT** Tools (this industry really likes felines). A Fuzzy Match is a TM segment that is partially related to the current segment you're working on. And how partially related it is can be depicted by a percentage rate ranging from 50% up to 99%. This means that the lower the percentage match the less stuff in common these segments will have, and vice versa. In other words, a low match percentage means more work for you, since you'll have to adjust accordingly the TM segment to the active document segment. Nevertheless, Fuzzy Matches in many cases speed-up your work since you'll quickly figure out the parts that need adjustment each time.

No Matches / New Words

This is the last match category which deals with, more or less, totally new words (a.k.a. No Matches). To be exact, the percentage match rate for this group is from 0% up to 49%. But due to the bad match quality, anything below 49% needs to be worked on from scratch, that's why it falls into the No Matches category.

It's worth noting here that many clients define the No Match category with a percentage rate of 0% - 74% (thus pushing the Fuzzy Match percentage range to 75% - 99%). This is good for you since it expands the No Match range, leading to more money in your pocket if you're applying a TM Match Discount Model.

Word Counts, The Trados Discount Model & Weighted Words

In the Translation Industry, the most frequently used method of quantifying the work involved is word counting. You should know, though, that there are also other measurement units such as lines and pages. But, if the project allows it, you'll nearly always see a word count mentioned in the project's details.

And, since we're talking about CAT Tools, word counts take a totally new twist here. Rather than simply counting total words in a file, CAT Tools allow for more in-depth statistics, such as Repetitions, 100% Matches, Context Matches, Fuzzy Matches and No Matches. These should all seem familiar to you by now, since we mentioned them further above as Translation Memory match categories. So, a TM serves another crucial purpose: It allows a comprehensive reporting of a project's translation status. In simpler words, we get a detailed picture of how much work is involved, or how much has been completed till this point. These statistics are usually called a TM Analysis or a TM Log, and are provided with every translation project that requires the use of a CAT Tool.

Below are two screenshots from TM Log examples:

Trados Studio Analysis Example:

Total	Type	Segments	Words	Characters
Files:3	PerfectMatch	0	0	0
Chars/Word:5.47	Context Match	3	15	78
	Repetitions	22	120	577
	Cross-file Repetitions	0	0	0
	100%	10	47	253
	95% - 99%	1	10	53
	85% - 94%	2	14	73
	75% - 84%	9	36	216
	50% - 74%	0	0	0
	New	131	748	4163
	Total	178	990	5413

Trados Studio Analysis

memoQ Analysis Example:

Type	Segments	Source words
All	1504	23767
X-translated / double context	0	0
Repetition	0	0
101%	0	0
100%	7	63
95%-99%	27	62
85%-94%	26	649
75%-84%	57	777
50%-74%	180	1237
No match	1207	20979

memoQ Analysis

In the above TM logs, you can see how it's possible to get an overview of a project's workload. Obviously, the more No Match words you have the more effort you'll be spending on the job. So with a simple glance at a TM log you can understand the project's difficulty and arrange your work time accordingly.

The Trados Discount Model

A side effect of the TM Analysis capability was the introduction by translation agencies of the Trados Discount Model. It was named that way for two reasons:

1. Trados Workbench was the dominant CAT Tool of that period.
2. It applied a discount payment based on TM Match categories.

Lately, you can also see it mentioned as the TM Match Discount Model, which better describes its purpose.

So, basically, this discount model does the following: It assigns different charging rates per TM Match category, allocating a full charging rate for No Matches and lowering that rate as the TM Matches move to Fuzzy Matches, 100% Matches and Repetitions. The concept behind this is that you work less on some TM Match categories than on others, so you should be paid accordingly.

Let me show you an example of such a TM Match Discount Model:

Match Category	Money Charge
Context Matches	0%
Repetitions	25%
100% Matches	25%
Fuzzy Matches	50%
No Matches	100%

The above table is one of the popular models applied by translation agencies, but you'll surely find a lot of variations to it.

Let me remind you that the Fuzzy Matches above contain the TM Match group of 75% - 99%, thus the No Matches above have a TM Match group of 0% - 74%. Don't confuse the TM Match percentage categories to the charging rate percentage! The first concerns TM Matches which is similarity of the segments, and the latter refers to payment percent per those TM Match categories.

You might be wondering why there's a 0% charge for the Context Matches and not at least a 25% charge as is the case with the 100% Matches in the above example. As explained earlier on, a Context Match is a "safe" 100% Match, which means it's bound to be correct and no further review or editing is required to it. In contrast with the 100% Matches, which need a quick review to ensure that their inline with the remaining context, thus the 25% payment for this effort.

Now let's see an actual example with a random word count and some money involved! We'll assume a rate of $0.10 per word and I'll use the full TM Match category breakdown. Also, I'll add an extra column titled "Calculation" so I can show you the behind-the-scenes math involved:

Match Category	Word Count	Money Charge	Calculation	Payment ($)
Context Matches	100	0%	(0 x 0.10) x 100	0
Repetitions	420	25%	(0.25 x 0.10) x 420	10.50
100% Matches	426	25%	(0.25 x 0.10) x 426	10.65
95% - 99% Matches	79	50%	(0.50 x 0.10) x 79	3.95
85% - 94% Matches	45	50%	(0.50 x 0.10) x 45	2.25
75% - 84% Matches	47	50%	(0.50 x 0.10) x 47	2.35
50% - 74% Matches	26	100%	(1.00 x 0.10) x 26	2.60

Match Category	Word Count	Money Charge	Calculation	Payment ($)
No Matches	3658	100%	(1.00 x 0.10) x 3658	365.80
Totals	4801	N/A	N/A	398.10

In the above example, we earn a total of $398.10 for this translation job. If the client hadn't requested the use of the TM Match Discount model (or hadn't required the use of a CAT Tool), the payment would've been $480.10 (4801 total words x $0.10 per word). But, you shouldn't feel cheated here. You might be working with a total of 4801 words, but the CAT Tool has relieved you of a lot of work when dealing with the Fuzzy and 100% Matches, as well as with the Repetitions. Plus, the Context Matches are a zero effort thing, since you don't have to touch them.

A lot of translators have expressed their hatred towards CAT Tools, and one key reason is the TM Match Discount Model. Having experienced this flame war both from the translator's and Project Manager's (a.k.a. client's) perspective, I have to say that there's no true ring to those allegations. Translation agencies are not out there planning sinister ways on how to steal every last cent from you. They have to apply such models when a CAT Tool is involved for various reasons, such as:

- Being more competitive: A saturated Translation Industry means less room for profits (a.k.a. sustainability) and, thus, the need for very competitive price offers to customers. Other than lowering the rate per word, which to be frank, cannot be lowered as much as needed, the alternative is applying the TM Match Discount Model. So this way, a translation agency can provide a viable price quote to a client while at the same time keeping the word rates at reasonable levels. This is a win-win situation for all parties involved (including, of course, you).

- Justification of work effort: Since the translation agency is providing you with a TM that contains various TM matches from previous work, your job has become quite easier as it's stepping on previous translations. Thus, with the help of your CAT Tool and the provided TM, your workload has been mitigated to levels that warrant such discounts.

So don't dismiss at first sight such deals with TM Match Discount Models. Keep an open mind, and just make sure that the proposed payment percentage rate per TM Match category is reasonable.

Weighted Words

Sometimes, it's quite handy to get an idea of a project's volume and its TM Match statistics just by looking at a single figure. It also uncomplicates the financial side of things, since only a single number has to be used and get multiplied by your word rate. That's where weighted word counts come in.

Weighted words have gained a lot of traction lately, and are provided along with the usual TM log so you can have the best possible picture of a project's volume. This magic number is achievable by applying a statistical formula to two key components: the charging rate percentage per TM Match category and the word count per that TM Match category. By multiplying these two components you get a weighted word count result.

Are you still with me? Let's put this into an example that will clarify things a bit. I'll use the same word count from the previous example:

Match Category	Money Charge	Word Count	Weighted Word Count
Context Matches	0%	100	0
Repetitions	25%	420	105
100% Matches	25%	426	106.5
95% - 99% Matches	50%	79	39.5
85% - 94% Matches	50%	45	22.5
75% - 84% Matches	50%	47	23.5
50% - 74% Matches	100%	26	26
No Matches	100%	3658	3658
Totals	**N/A**	**4801**	**3981**

So by applying the simple formula **[Money Charge Rate]** x **[Word Count]** per TM Match category we get a weighted word count per that TM Match category, and by adding them all up you obtain that precious single figure we're talking about all this time.

Now let's verify what we've said earlier on, that if you multiply the weighted word count by your translation word rate you will get the project's total cost. I'll juxtapose the numbers from the first example so we can make the comparison easier:

Example 1 Results:

Project Cost: $398.10
Calculation Method: TM Log

Example 2 Results:

Project Cost: $398.10
Calculation Method: Weighted word count x word rate (3981 x 0.10)

No surprises here. The project's cost matches in both cases.

Note that weighted words can only exist when using a CAT Tool. This should be obvious to you by now, since the components for calculating a weighted word count rely on TM Match categories.

Terminology Databases (TermBases)

As we have said earlier in this guide, a Terminology Database's functionality is quite similar to a TM's, with the main difference being that TermBases accumulate only specific, predefined keywords/phrases labeled as terms (short for terminology). These terms are stored in a multilingual format and may be accompanied by the following information:

- Unique ID number
- Definition
- Context of the term
- Subject field
- Grammar description (i.e., verb, noun, etc.)
- Creation/Modification time-stamp
- etc.

Let's see an actual screenshot from SDL Trados Studio 2014 that shows a TermBase in action:

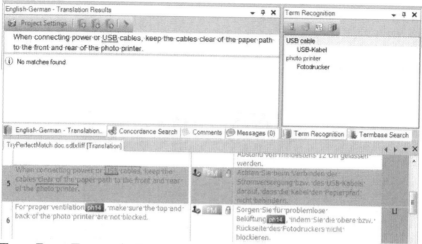

TermBase Example 1

It's clear that in segment 5 the CAT Tool has identified two terms: "USB Cable" and "photo printer". It has placed a red line over these words (in the source segment) to denote their importance. If you look at the top right corner of our screenshot, you'll see that the connected TermBase has provided the corresponding translations for these two terms. It should be clear now how helpful a Termbase can be, especially when dealing with tough technical translations.

Furthermore, you can view any extra information provided with these terms in the TermBase by using the applicable method for your CAT Tool (in our case by clicking the icon with the magnifying glass in the TermBase pane toolbar). This action displays the following on our screen:

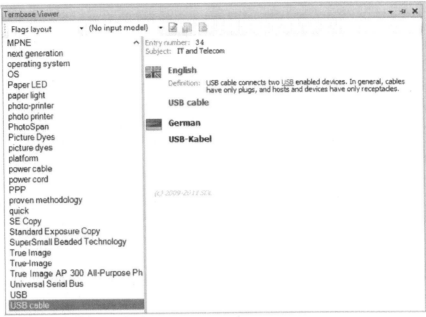

TermBase Example 2

On the left pane is a list of supported terms and on the right pane is their detailed information. In our case, we learn that "USB cable" has an entry number of 34, has a definition we can read about and is related to the "IT and Telecom" subject field. And, needless to say, we're also provided with the translation of the term.

I highly advise using a TermBase whenever possible. In most cases, the client will be providing you with one, especially if the project involves any type of serious technical translation work.

Handoff & Delivery Packages

Before we delve into a typical translation project workflow, which is our next topic, I'd like to say a few things about the new methods CAT Tools have devised to simplify the assignment and return of translation tasks.

In this case, a translation task is a subset of a translation project. Depending on the project's scope, we could have many translation tasks and in many target languages, all within this same project. In the past, this was a problem for Project Managers as CAT Tools didn't have an easy way of bundling such tasks together for dispatching them to a translator. They had to manually separate some files, analyze them with the TM, zip everything up and send by email to the translator, crossing their fingers in the process. And, as you might have guessed, what the translators returned back was also a tricky situation, as they often forgot to include crucial files or notes with the delivery, or even sent back wrong files. Now imagine this process for a large project with many translators involved. This was indeed a Project Manager's hell on earth.

The solution came, obviously, from the CAT Tool developers. They started including task management features in their software which allowed users (Project Managers and translators) to handle smoothly translation task assignments and deliveries (a.k.a. packages). Let's briefly check out these features.

Handoff Packages

Depending on the CAT Tool, you could see them referred to as Project Packages as well.

Someone, usually a Project Manager from a translation agency, when starting the Handoff Package creation process, selects the appropriate tasks he/she wishes to assign from the CAT Tool's project dashboard. There are nifty options available for this process too: the Project Manager can choose to select individual files or base his/her selection on word count (i.e., preparing a package with specific volume), plus some other options as well.

Once the selection is done, the files/parts involved are marked internally by the CAT Tool as unavailable so there's no double assigning of the same material. The Project Manager is also requested by the process to indicate any extra material, such as TM and TermBase inclusion or even reference files. Once everything's ready, the CAT Tool generates a single file, the so-called Handoff Package which can now be emailed to the translator.

So, in a typical Handoff Package we should find the following:

- Working files (source files specially prepared for translation)
- Translation Memory
- TermBase (if applicable)
- TM Analysis Report (contains the TM Match statistics)
- Reference material (if applicable)
- Deadline and other information

Technically, though, you won't be able to see any of the above unless you open the Handoff Package in your CAT Tool. And, your CAT Tool should be compatible with the one that created the package (lately, all major CAT Tools seem to support each other's packages so you could, in theory, use a different tool). So, once opened, the package will automatically set up the project's environment and activate the necessary TM and TermBase. It will also set the deadline in your CAT Tool, so you can see how much time there's left before delivery.

It's worth noting here that the ability to create Handoff Packages is usually limited to the high-end CAT Tool versions, which are usually more expensive to purchase and are generally used by translation agencies.

Delivery Packages

These are also known as Return Packages, depending on the CAT Tool platform. Unlike the process involved with Handoff Packages, Delivery Packages are quite straightforward to create. So, once a translator is done with the work, he/she has to simply select the relevant button or menu option that will create the Delivery/Return Package for the project he/she was working on. Usually, there are no options to set here, so the translator will end up with a single file that he/she can send back to the client.

This Delivery Package will contain all necessary items which the Project Manager needs, and these will be automatically imported into his project once he/she opens the Delivery Package in the CAT Tool.

It should be evident by now how packages have made everyone's life easier. So don't run away if you're confronted with these file types, and be sure to ask for them when your client doesn't provide them up-front.

A Typical Translation Project Workflow

Now that we've learned about CAT Tools and their components, it's time to show how a regular translation project is handled with these tools. And since this is a translator's guide, we'll be looking into this mostly from the translator's perspective.

Client Handoff

This is where it all starts. After confirming your availability, the job's deadline and word rate, the client proceeds and sends you the translation project. Depending on your client's background, the handoff will contain one of the following:

- Direct source files
- CAT Tool Files or Handoff Package

If the client isn't a translation agency then most probably you'll receive direct source files and some reference material (i.e., similar or older translated documents). In this case, the client isn't aware of any TM Match Discount Models (or anything related to CAT Tools), so you could take advantage of the situation by using your CAT Tool to translate this project, earning more money with less effort (remember, you'll be paid for total words but you'll be working less thanks to Fuzzy Matches, 100% Matches and Repetitions).

On the other hand, if your client is a translation agency then you'll surely receive files prepared for translation in a CAT Tool. These could be either pre-processed CAT Tool files along with a TM and TermBase, or a simple Handoff Package which, as we've seen, is a neat bundle with everything included for your work. This type of client, of course, will request the application of a TM Match Discount Model, but you'll know that from the start since you'll have to agree to it along with the word rate.

Keep in mind though that, lately, a lot of companies that aren't translation agencies have started using CAT Tools in their corporate translation requirements. The benefits are obvious to them now: translation and terminology consistency, translation re-cycling, easier project management, lower costs and so on. For example, companies such as Coca-Cola, General Electric, Sony, ExxonMobil are using Wordfast, the CAT Tool we described earlier on in **CAT Tools Panorama!** So don't be surprised if a new client with no affiliations to a translation agency starts asking for TM Match Discount Models.

Let's see now how you'll be handling each client handoff case when using a CAT Tool.

Direct Source Files

When we refer to source files, we're talking about original, unprocessed documents. These could be of any type such as: MS Word (.doc/.docx), MS Excel (.xls/.xlsx), MS PowerPoint (.ppt/.pptx), Adobe Acrobat (.pdf), Adobe InDesign (.indd/.idml), Rich Text Format (.rtf), Text file (.txt), Html (.htm) and so on. The list isn't endless, though. Each CAT Tool supports a specific number of source file formats, but in general, you'll be glad to know that all major source file formats are supported and you'll rarely face a situation in which your source file is unsupported.

So in this handoff case, where a client sends you source files, your first action should be to import them into your CAT Tool. Then, and if not already done, you should either create a new, blank TM and TermBase or hook up an existing TM and TermBase. At this stage you should run the pre-translation process offered by your CAT Tool on the files, which will automatically translate the 100% Matches and Context Matches, if available in the TM. This will save you time when dealing with those TM Match categories. At this point, it's good to do a TM Analysis on the imported files; the resulting report will give you an idea of the actual work involved, taking into consideration any TM Matches available by the TM.

An outline of the above described process is as follows:

1. Import source files
2. Attach blank or existing TM and TermBase
3. Pre-Translate files
4. Run a TM Analysis

Note: To avoid nasty surprises, I highly suggest you attempt to generate the target files at this stage, in their current untranslated (or partially translated) condition (see **Delivery / Handback** further down this guide). This way, you can find out in advance if there are problems with the target file generation process. I've encountered a lot of instances where translators couldn't create the target files after painstakingly translating a large project.

CAT Tool Files Or Handoff Package

Things get quite easier when your client handoffs processed CAT Tool files or, even better, a Handoff Package. Here, most of the steps outlined in the previous section have already been applied, and the ones pending can be easily dealt with.

If you receive CAT Tool files, these will include the following parts:

- CAT Tool processed files
- Translation Memory
- TermBase (optional)
- TM Analysis Report

What's left for you to do is to insert the files in your CAT Tool and attach to them the provided TM and TermBase. From here on you're ready to go!

In the case of a Handoff Package, there's practically nothing for you to do other than opening it in your CAT Tool. Everything will be automatically set up for you, thanks to CAT Tool Package technology.

Translation

Eventually, you'll have to start translating, right? This is where you'll be applying your own language skills to the project. And since you're using a CAT Tool, you'll be aided by all those nifty features that come with it and which we've described further above. But, there are some extra tips you can follow that will make the translation process a bit easier, or at least less frustrating. Let me mention the most useful.

Invisible Characters

As the name suggests, these are characters that aren't visible by default. The most common non-visible characters are spaces (a.k.a. whitespaces), tabs and paragraph marks. You may be acquainted with these in MS Word, which has a similar option to show or hide invisible characters. Let's have a look at two screenshots that show how a segment appears with and without invisible characters:

Screenshot 1: Without invisible characters (default)

```
      They are useful for
      the big picture, but they don't get into details in the same way as
      more specific topics.</p></body>
      <topic>
80    <title>A specific topic</title>
      <shortdesc>This is a more specific topic.</shortdesc>
      <body><p>Specifically, this is more specific.</p></body>
      </topic>
      </topic>
```

Without Invisible Characters

Screenshot 2: With invisible characters

```
      They·are·useful·for¶
      ··the·big·picture,·but·they·don't·get·into·details·in·the·same·way·as¶
      ··more·specific·topics.</p></body>¶
      ··<topic>¶
80    ····<title>A·specific·topic</title>¶
      ····<shortdesc>This·is·a·more·specific·topic.</shortdesc>¶
      ····<body><p>Specifically,·this·is·more·specific.</p></body>¶
      ··</topic>¶
      </topic>
```

With Invisible Characters

As you can see in screenshot 2, things get quite interesting when showing invisible characters. All of a sudden, you have a clear picture of how each sentence is formatted, how many spaces are between words, where new lines start and whether there are tabs or not. This makes things easier when trying to follow the same formatting in the target segment, the one in which you'll be inserting your translation.

At first, you may get distracted by the extra symbols appearing in your text, but you'll quickly get used to them. I highly suggest you enable showing invisible characters in your CAT Tool, something that all professional translators do nowadays. Look for the ¶ symbol (paragraph mark) in your CAT Tool toolbar or find the appropriate option in the menus to enable this feature.

Tags

When dealing with complicated source files like XML, HTML, InDesign INDD/IDML, Java Resources etc., a CAT Tool has to make sure you're not exposed to parts that aren't meant to be touched. These parts are usually computer code, or special formatting settings native only to the software that created the source file. If these get modified for any reason then there might be unforeseen consequences, like not being able to generate the final translated file (a.k.a. target file), or the final file being a mess in terms of layout and fonts just to name a few. For these reasons the CAT Tool identifies these sensitive parts and replaces them with tags which appear like small triangles or rectangles in segments.

We should mention here that tags have become quite prevalent in the last years, so you'll also see them appearing in your Editor when dealing with MS Office files too. Again, these tags represent special formatting instructions that shouldn't be modified, hence their replacement with tags in the segments.

Here's a screenshot showing what tags look like in a CAT Tool Editor:

This conference presents the new ▶education *programme*◀ unveiled by the Minister for Education last year.

▶**For more information**◀, contact your local branch of the Teachers Education Programme Foundation◀.

▶**Collect the conference motor car mascots**◀ for your school.

Register today and obtain a ▶**20% discount**◀!

Tags

All those purple objects in the screenshot are tags.

If you're curious to see what's in those tags, you can do that by enabling the relevant tag view option in your CAT Tool. In most cases, you'd be looking for the "Full Tag Text" view. If we enable it, here's how the previous screenshot looks like:

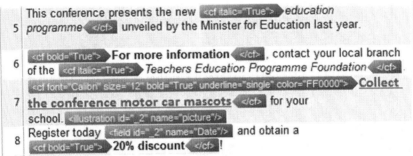

Tags - Full View

Quite intimidating, right? That's the reason for tags, so you don't have to stare at that stuff during your translation work.

But, tags can prove a hassle if not handled in the right way. So, here are some tips to take full advantage of them:

1. Make sure you enable a tag view that allows numbering of the tags. This is the best view mode since you can easily insert in the correct order the tags in your target segment.
2. Include the same tags present in the source segment into your target segment. Make sure these are the same in terms of tag number and position.

3. Identify all tag mismatches, which are wrongly placed tags. It's very important these are fixed otherwise you might not be able to generate your target file, or if you can generate it, the formatting will surely have issues.

Segment Status

The segment status represents the translation condition of a segment. In short, it shows whether it's translated or not. But since we're talking about CAT Tools, things get more interesting thanks to the introduction of various statuses that pretty much describe the same thing, albeit in a slightly different way.

The good thing is we can use these segment statuses for our own purposes, allowing for a better and more efficient management of our translations. First, let me present the most common statuses (names may vary slightly per CAT Tool):

- Not Translated
- Draft
- Translated
- Translation Approved

So, we actually have one status (Not Translated) describing an untranslated segment, and three statuses labeling a segment as translated! Boy, they really want to make sure a segment is translated.

Now let me show you how I'd use these statuses to make sense of my in-progress translation work. I'll describe how I'd mark a segment based on its condition:

Not Translated: This one is pretty obvious. All untranslated segments will have this status automatically. I'd also revert a segment (or a group of segments) and mark them as "Not Translated" if required for some reason (i.e., really bad or totally wrong translation and so on).

Draft: This status will automatically be applied once you translate a segment. So, I'd leave it at this status until I have a chance to read it again (proofread). I'd also mark any other segment as "Draft" if I'm not sure about the translation quality, or if I need to go over it one more time.

Translated: I'd mark segments as "Translated" once they have been proofread by me. This way I'll know that the translation quality if final from my side.

Translation Approved: I'd use this status for segments that previously had a "Translated" status and have been proofread and finalized by another person (i.e., a colleague, a client and so on).

Once you start applying the above status assigning model, you'll quickly have a better understanding of your translation progress and can easily shift your focus on the required parts of your work.

Concordance Search

More often than not, you'll end up in a situation that requires searching the active TM for a word or phrase to see how it has already been translated. The easiest way to accomplish this is by using the Concordance Search feature. You can activate this search function either by selecting it from your CAT Tool's toolbar, or by locating it in the relevant menu. The results from such a search show you the source and target translations that contain the word or phrase you're looking for.

Most incarnations of the Concordance Search allow for searching in both source and target segments which can be quite handy in many cases. Also, most CAT Tools allow you to highlight the word/phrase and then right-click on it, which will bring up a context menu that includes the Concordance Search option.

If you're not using this search feature then you should reconsider. Concordance Search is a quick method to retain consistency and find how an unknown term has been translated in the past.

Handling Repetitions

As we've stated earlier on, Repetitions are identical, untranslated segments that repeat themselves in a file. You might be wondering why we're dealing with them again here. Well, there are a couple of tricks you can do that will make handling Repetitions a lot easier, not to mention a lot more efficient. This is all useful, of course, when you have a project with a reasonable number of Repetitions.

The theory is to isolate the unique Repetitions (a.k.a. first occurrences) and display only these for translation. Once these get translated your CAT Tool will auto-propagate the translations to the remaining occurrences, thus eliminating them from your workload. You can apply either one of these tricks, depending on which feels more natural to your process.

Filtered View

Most modern CAT Tools support filtered views in their Editors. If your does too, enable a view that shows only the unique Repetitions, or their first occurrences. You can now focus on this small number of segments and go through them quickly. Once done, you remove the filter and return to your normal Editor view.

Locking Segments

If filtered views aren't your thing because segments appear out of context, then you can apply this slightly tedious alternative method. Enable a filtered view, or apply the corresponding process, for displaying all non-unique Repetitions, or Repetitions excluding their first occurrence. Then select all these segments and apply the corresponding locking process allowed by your CAT Tool (in most tools, you can simply right-click these selected segments and select "Lock Segment" or choose the equivalent option). Now remove the filtered view. You'll be back to your normal Editor view and can resume your translation. Since the non-unique Repetitions are locked, you will be dealing with the first occurrences only. When done translating the file, enable the non-unique Repetitions filtered view again and unlock these segments. Apply your CAT Tool's pre-translation process on the file and all non-unique Repetitions will be translated.

Obviously, the second method is a bit more complicated to apply but has the benefit of displaying all segments in context (i.e., in their natural order).

Proofreading & Spell-Checking

I know this should be apparent, but you'll be surprised how many translators (yes, even experienced ones) neglect proofreading and/or spell-checking their finished work. Even if your client will be proofreading your translation afterwards, there's no reason for you to deliver an unchecked work. If you pick up this bad habit, then I can guarantee you'll see a steady decrease of projects coming your way. You should always consider your completed translation as text ready to be published.

Regarding proofreading, the process is quite straightforward. After you've translated your project, you do a second pass reading everything and correcting the evident errors. If you've applied my suggested model of Segment Statuses, then you should filter for "Draft" segments and start reading them. Once you proofread each segment you should change the status to "Translated" (or after proofreading all "Draft" segments, select them all and change their status to "Translated").

Sometimes, even proofreading your own work isn't enough to catch all errors. This is normal since humans have a tendency to ignore things for which they're sure are okay, even if these errors are practically screaming in front of them. That's why most translation agencies always have a proofreader or reviewer go over your work. This isn't an excuse for you not proofreading your work, though!

The spell-checking process found in modern CAT Tool software has improved a lot in recent years. It can now distinguish different languages within a segment, highlight errors and suggest possible corrections, learn from your errors and so on. So, why on earth wouldn't you want to apply this to your translation? To be frank, it's the least you can do before sending your work to the client. I can tell you that clients will be lenient for a few proofreading errors, but will be enraged with a lot of spelling mistakes. You have been warned.

Verification Checks

Another important check you should do before delivering is the Verification Check, which is available in most modern CAT Tools (the name may vary). This process scrutinizes your work in three main areas: Quality Assurance (QA), Terminology and Tags. Let's see what each area has to offer.

Quality Assurance (QA) Area

This area covers errors that can be overlooked during the proofreading and spell-checking phases. It also identifies possible problems that can't be discovered by a translator when dealing with multiple files. Here are a few of the checks applied by the QA process:

- **Inconsistency check:** Identifies source or target inconsistencies, which are different translations of the same source or target segment.
- **Punctuation check:** Indicates punctuation discrepancies between source and target segments.
- **Numbers check:** Locates numerical, date and time discrepancies between source and target segments. It can also be used to identify unlocalized versions of these as well.
- **Trademark check:** If applicable, will check against the project's Trademark List and indicate which trademarks have or haven't been translated.
- **Character length limit check:** If applicable, will check each segment against the project's Character Length Limit values and identify possible problems.

Terminology Area

The Terminology area concentrates on making sure the predefined terms from the TermBase are correctly applied in your translation. Of course, this is only applicable when you have an active TermBase attached to your project. Moreover, this area also checks for banned terms, which are terms that shouldn't appear in the target segment.

Tags Area

When dealing with files that have tags, this check will save you from a lot of hair-pulling moments. As has been mentioned, tags can be blamed for errors during target file generation and, in general, problematic target files. Here are a few of what gets checked in this area:

- Extra, moved or deleted tags
- Wrong tag sequence
- Tag discrepancy in source and target segments
- Corrupt tags

So, save your sanity and include a Verification Check before you send the files to your client.

Delivery / Handback

Eventually, the time will come to deliver your work to the client. Depending on the method of the client's handoff, there might be some extra steps you should follow before sending the project. Let's have a look at each possible handback process.

Direct Target Files

If you were provided with direct source files, then most likely your client doesn't use CAT Tools, so you should deliver to them the translated equivalent of these files: direct target files. This is easily accomplished by applying the corresponding process from within your CAT Tool. Look for options (either in your tool's menus or toolbar) that mention "Save as target", "Save target translation", or anything similar. If you're handling a single file, then this could be done from within the CAT Tool's Editor too, usually when accessing the "File" menu.

Once the target files have been generated it's good practice to open them in their corresponding software (i.e., MS Word when dealing with .doc/.docx file and so on), and have a quick look at the translated content. Sometimes, you may need to make some cosmetic adjustments or corrections which only become evident when viewing the file in its original environment. Of course, this won't be always possible, especially when dealing with obscure source files; so if you double-click the target file and it doesn't open don't fret. Let the client deal with it.

CAT Tool Files Or Delivery Package

If, on the other hand, your client uses a CAT Tool then you surely received either CAT Tool files along with a TM and TermBase (optional), or a Handoff Package. In each case the delivery should comply with the client's expectations, so let me outline what that means per case.

CAT Tool Files Delivery

Here you should prepare a proper delivery that consists of the following items:

- Translated CAT Tool Files (a.k.a. bilingual files)
- Generated target files
- TM (or TM export)
- TermBase (or TermBase export)

The exports mentioned for the TM and Termbase are optional, and should be considered only when the client requests such files. For reference, a TM export is usually called a TMX file (Translation Memory eXchange) and a TermBase export is called a TBX file (TermBase eXchange). Most modern CAT Tools allow exporting in these formats, so you should be okay if you're asked to provide them (consult your CAT Tool's online manual for more details).

Note that in some cases, you won't be able to generate the target files. This is often true when a client provides CAT Tool files only (without any direct source files). CAT Tools are picky in this sense, and prefer to generate target files from the same computer that prepared the bilingual files (CAT Tool files). So don't worry if you come by such issues, and just make sure to report it to the client.

It's worth reminding you here the importance of verifying the files prior to generating the target files. So, run the Verification Check and correct all necessary reported errors. Special care must be given to tag issues; as we said earlier on, tags can block the target file generation process.

Delivery Package

As with Handoff Packages, there's practically not much to do here to prepare a Delivery Package. Your CAT Tool takes care of everything, so you only have to instruct it to initiate the process. You can find this option in your tool's toolbar or menu. The end result will be a Delivery Package that you can then send to the client. It doesn't get simpler than that!

Of course, to be able to deliver such a package, you need to have received a Handoff Package from the client which will instruct your CAT Tool how to generate the Delivery Package when that time comes.

Machine Translation (MT)

Machine Translation (MT) should not be confused with a Translation Memory (TM), or with any other CAT Tool aspect. As stated in the beginning of this part, a CAT Tool is a Computer-Assisted Translation Tool, which means a human translator needs to be involved. You could imagine a CAT Tool being a translator's utility belt. It's his/her instrument that allows for quick and efficient translation of projects. In other words, the human does all the mental work, not the tool.

On the other hand, MT is pure computer involvement, with no human interaction during the process (a human can check and correct the MT segments later on, of course). MT isn't magic and isn't perfect yet, but for specific translation areas and language combinations the results are quite good. MT is possible using various algorithm approaches, two of which have gained more traction in recent years:

- Rule-based approach
- Statistical approach

A rule-based approach, as the name implies, uses a set of rules which instruct the MT process how to deal with the translation. These rules involve language and grammar style, and added to the mix are special dictionaries to assist the process when dealing with specialized industry terminology.

A statistical approach has nothing to do with a language's grammar, syntax or style. It acquires knowledge of a language by examining volumes of data (a.k.a. corpus) for the specific language pairs.

The reason we're mentioning MT here is because all modern CAT Tools support them as add-ons or plugins. So, in theory, you could hook-up one of them and have it machine translate your work. But, there's a catch. The resulting MT quality varies considerably depending on the language pair and subject field of your project. This means you'll be spending a considerable time reviewing these MT segments and, in most cases, either correcting or re-translating them. So, what had started as a time-saving idea, could end up costing you your deadline and sanity.

But, MT can be worth it when dealing with specific language pairs and domains. And the best way to find out if an MT translation suits your needs is by applying it to a copy of your project. If the results are good enough for you (meaning you need to apply minimum changes to the resulting MT segments), then you can apply it to your main project. Otherwise, just skip the process entirely and focus on your work as usual.

We should note here that the best MT add-ons/plugins aren't free. They require either a monthly subscription fee, or a fee per a specific volume of MT translation.

Avoiding CAT Tool Lock-In

A CAT Tool Lock-In is the situation in which you're forced to use a specific CAT Tool because all your previous work is tied to that platform. This used to be the case in past years, where CAT Tools where trying to gain traction by locking in users, forcing them to pay for every next major upgrade. The good thing is we're seeing less and less of this tactic being upheld by major CAT Tool developers today. Nonetheless, the danger still exists.

It should be made clear that the lock-in is done on these three levels:

- Bilingual files (a.k.a. CAT Tool files)
- Translation Memory (TM)
- TermBase

You can see we're talking here about a total lock-in. The bad news is that we can't free all three levels. The good news is that we can unshackle the last two levels (TM & TermBase), which thankfully include all your translation work, including that present in the doomed bilingual files. And, just so you know, the TMs and TermBases, but especially the TMs, are the files that contain all your work. So our focus would've been on these either way.

So, how can you avoid such a scenario? And, if you're already in such a situation, how can you lead your existing locked-in work to freedom? Let me show you how.

Freeing Past & Existing Translations

Depending on how old your past work is will define the proper freeing action. The reason is simple: older work means use of older CAT Tools which tried their best to lock you in as tight as possible. So, most probably, that old CAT Tool, assuming you still have access to it, doesn't have an option to export in any industry standard format such as TMX (for TMs) and TBX (for TermBases). In this case, we'll use the same CAT Tool against its own self. To be more precise, we'll use a newer version of it for our cause.

Since you're in a CAT Tool lock-in, chances are you already have the newest version of that tool. Even if you haven't upgraded, you surely will find a colleague with a newer version that will assist you. So, the trick here is to use the export feature from the newer CAT Tool, and convert all your TMs and TermBases to TMX and TBX format. Each new CAT Tool version will always support its pervious lock-in formats, so we're taking advantage of that feature (a.k.a. backward compatibility).

Now you're free to use your freshly exported TMXs and TBXs in any modern CAT Tool environment.

Keeping Your Future Work Cross-Platform

In contrast with their older incarnations, today's CAT Tools have wisely chosen to include export features to all major industry standard formats. Furthermore, they've also started including partial support for bilingual open standards, such as XLIFF, which cracks a bit more the lock-in wall for that type of format. But, the danger is still present.

For these reasons, a wise option for you would be to create frequent exports of your working TMs and TermBases. These exports should be in TMX (for TMs) and TBX (for TermBases) for maximum compatibility between CAT Tools. Once you have a process like this set up, you'll be free to use any CAT Tool platform available, and avoid the pitfalls of a CAT Tool lock-in.

CAT Tools On A Mac Or GNU/Linux

If you would've asked me in the recent past whether it was worth running your translation business off a Mac or a GNU/Linux system, I'd quickly (and without second thoughts) have instructed you to forget about it. And this was an obvious, cruel fact back then. Thankfully, this isn't the case anymore.

Recent technological advances, in both hardware and software, have opened the door to multiple options for you to run your favorite CAT Tool on a Mac or GNU/Linux system. Taking for example the Mac platform, Apple's switch of CPU (Central Processing Unit) architecture in their Mac line of computers from PowerPC to Intel-based chips allowed the platform to support, directly or by virtualization, all modern CAT Tools. This specific switch even made it possible to run natively Microsoft Windows on a Mac! And if you're wondering, no, hell hasn't frozen over... yet.

Let's have a look at the available options, and what their pros and cons are.

Native CAT Tools

When we refer to native CAT Tools, or any software in this context, we mean computer programs that have been created for a specific operating system. And since Microsoft Windows was (and still is) the dominant platform, the majority of CAT Tools have been developed for this operating system only.

Recently however, this has changed in favor of the second and third most popular operating systems: Mac OS X and GNU/Linux. Some true CAT Tool alternatives to the heavyweights have been developed for these platforms, attempting to match the features offered in them. And at least one of the big players, Wordfast, has managed to add support for all three operating systems.

The benefits of native software are quite evident and include:

- Faster loading and response times
- Familiar and consistent user interface
- Finer integration with other native software
- A solid working environment

If you'd like to see what CAT Tools are native to your platform, check out section **CAT Tools Panorama!** further above which highlights some popular CAT Tools for use in your translation business. Of course, you can (and should) search in your preferred search engine too, for any additional CAT Tools available for your operating system.

Mac & MS Windows via Boot Camp

Since you can run Microsoft Windows natively on a Mac (by using Apple's included Boot Camp setup tool), it deserves a mention here. If you don't mind dual booting between OS X and MS Windows, then you can take advantage of such a setup. But, you need to know the following:

- Installing MS Windows on a Mac via Boot Camp requires a valid MS Windows license. This means you're practically purchasing an operating system.
- If you need any extra proprietary software, then you'll need to purchase the MS Windows version, regardless if you have the OS X version (exceptions apply here depending on software company).
- While booted in MS Windows, you cannot access any information or apps on your OS X system. You can however view the OS X files and folders and manipulate them (with caution!).
- Your Mac will be vulnerable to viruses and malware if no proper antivirus protection is taken when running in MS Windows.

If you're still okay with the above points, then you can proceed and purchase any MS Windows supported CAT Tool and run it natively in your Boot Camp partition.

Virtualized CAT Tools

With modern computer systems getting cheaper and more powerful, another option became available to users that needed to run non-native software on their computers. Described as Software Virtualization, this process allows the creation of Virtual Machines (VMs) in which you can install and run your chosen operating system and, on top of that, the required software (i.e., in our case, CAT Tools).

So, basically, you'll run a Virtual Machine like any other software on your computer, with the difference that, inside it, you'll be running another operating system along with the required apps! If you're thinking this looks like those Russian Matryoshka dolls, then you're right. Your computer is actually emulating another computer, and it's doing this concurrently. It may sound a bit schizophrenic, but it's very practical.

This means that you can multi-task your way around both systems (virtualized and actual) and share files and information too. You have the benefits of both worlds on a single machine, and in real-time.

For GNU/Linux systems, the two easiest and popular options for virtualization include VirtualBox and VMWare Workstation. VirtualBox (https://www.virtualbox.org) is a free Open Source virtualization software that's supported by Oracle. It's a great compromise between cost (nothing beats free!) and functionality. It can feel a bit rough on the edges, but its latest versions have moved it closer to the competition in terms of features and speed. VMWare Workstation (http://www.vmware.com/products/workstation/) is a proprietary virtualization solution, and can be considered one of the best for this job. You won't be surprised to learn that the company behind this software, VMWare Inc., started this whole virtualization craze in the first place, being the first software company to create and commercialize the virtualization of the x86 architecture (Intel's CPUs). So, a safe bet would be using VMWare Workstation, especially if you're not too computer-savvy.

If you're on a Mac, you have three popular virtualization software options. The first is VirtualBox, the same software mentioned above. The second one is again from VMWare Inc., but it's the Mac version which is called VMWare Fusion (https://www.vmware.com/products/fusion). And the third solution is Parallels Desktop (http://www.parallels.com/products/desktop/), a Mac-only virtualization solution from Parallels IP Holdings GmbH. All three can be used, but from personal experience (yes, I'm a Mac user!) I think Parallels Desktop has a slight winning edge over the other two, with VMWare Fusion following very close behind. If you're a typical Mac user, you'll find Parallels Desktop's way of doing things more natural to your workflow on OS X.

I should make clear here that in order to have a smooth experience with any of the mentioned virtualization software, your computer system must be a relatively recent model. If it's not that new, then you could try adding some extra memory (RAM) and switching from a traditional hard disk to a Solid State Disk (SSD). That should help considerably and allow you to work without problems in your VM.

Part 3: Running A Freelance Translation Business

In this part of the guide I'll provide you with very useful information on how to successfully run your freelance business. You'll be presented with "inside" information on how clients (especially translation agencies) choose their translators. You'll learn how to set up profiting rates and how to find promising clients. I'll give you ideas for efficient organization of your work process and tips for successful customer relationship management. Oh, and I'll show you how to stay away from fraudulent companies, too. All this and much more follow in this interesting part!

Defining Your Core Language Pairs

You're reading this guide because you're bilingual and interested in making a living (or some extra cash) by translating. For a successful start, though, you need to make sure you define correctly the language pairs you'll be working with.

For example, if your language pair is English and German, you need to decide on the direction of translation for these languages. Is it English into German (English => German) or, maybe, German into English (German => English)? Is it both ways (English <=> German)? This is very important as it will define the quality and word throughput of your work, for the simple reason that, most often, we're more fluent in one language than the other. Of course, it's quite normal to be fluent in many languages in which case you can define both directions of translation (lucky you!).

In the translation industry, we use the terms source language and target language to define the direction of a translation. Moreover, the target language is assumed (or mandated) to be the translator's mother tongue, securing this way a native quality translation. As for the source language, the requirements are less strict on the translator, and simply demand a very good comprehension of it. This allows for multiple source language coverage, since someone can comprehend more than one language. So, using our language example above, if you're good with French too and your mother tongue is German, you could declare the following language pairs:

Source Language	Target Language
English	German
French	German

So take your time when deciding your working language pairs. If you're quite confident with either language direction then, by all means, include both pairs in your pitch to the client. Otherwise, stick to the single or two pairs that make you most comfortable.

Setting Up Your Pricelist

This is where things get serious and tricky at the same time. Your pricelist (a.k.a. word rate) is the most crucial aspect of your translation business. You need to find the magic number that will allow clients to provide you with a steady flow of work. If you place your rates at the higher end you risk losing or receiving less work. On the other hand, if you go too low, you'll receive too much work without the corresponding compensation for your effort; and, you also risk being rejected by some clients who believe cheap rates are an indication of low quality work.

If you're already a translator, you should know by now what are the normal price ranges for your language pair. If you're just now starting out in this business, though, you'll be glad to know that I'll provide you with some rate ranges that will allow you to get moving until you can refine them later on, once you obtain some experience.

But before we delve into actual word rates, I'd like to give you this "inside" advice concerning rates and clients: Depending on the type of client, it's possible to assign different rates for the same language pair. Read on to learn how this works.

Rates For Translation Agencies

When your client is a translation agency, you have to understand the following:

- They act as the intermediary between you and the direct customer.
- They have won the contract (a.k.a. work) from the customer, meaning they did all the sales push and effort to accomplish this.
- They need to make a profit.
- They can use another translator, if needed.
- They can provide a steady flow of work.

The above points simply state the fact that a translation agency is a very good client to work with, and that you should cut them some slack when negotiating rates. I'm not suggesting here for you to accept any unreasonable rate agreement, but to be more down-to-earth when dealing with them. A translation agency has lots of work to offer and in high frequency. If you get rolling with them, most likely you'll be turning jobs down due to overloading than asking for more work. They cover all the difficult tasks such as customer acquisition, project preparation, project checks and delivery to the customer. You're left to focus on your core translation service.

For these reasons, when negotiating prices with a translation agency you should aim at the lower end of your word rate range. You'll surely benefit from this and see some great financial results quickly enough.

Note: Nearly all translation agencies will require you to use some kind of CAT Tool. Moreover, they'll surely ask you to agree to a TM Match Discount Model, which varies per agency. But, you shouldn't be concerned here since most models are pretty reasonable, so there's no reason fretting over it and risk losing a good translation job.

Rates For Direct (Non-Agency) Customers

In contrast to a translation agency, a direct (non-agency) customer is quite a catch if, that is, you manage to get hold of one. Unlike translation agencies which actively seek out translators for their projects, direct customers usually don't have a process set up when dealing with translation requirements in their company. They usually don't post translation requests at online translation forums, or roam the relevant translation websites in search for translators. They usually assign this process to an unlucky internal employee (office manager or secretary) and he/she does his/her best to find a translator by asking around or looking online.

The above is true for small translation tasks, though. If large or multi-language translation volumes are involved, then you could pretty much say goodbye to any potential work coming your way, at least directly. The reason is, they'll be forced to look at agency options because of the volume.

On the other hand, if you do manage to acquire a direct customer then the benefits far outnumber the troubles you went through to accomplish this. For starters, a direct customer isn't concerned much about word rates as he is about translation quality. And, most of the time, a direct customer doesn't even know what a word rate is, even less so what a good word rate looks like! This gives you enough room for increasing your rate considerably. But, you need to be reasonable. That's why I'd suggest an increase of your standard word rate within a range of 40% to 80%. That's quite a good range to maneuver in and keep the direct customer happy.

Secondly, as we've noted in this guide, a direct customer most times doesn't know about or use CAT Tools. This gives you another leverage, since you can take advantage of any Repetition Matches and, once you've done some translation work for them, the Fuzzy and 100% Matches as well. This way you'll boost your profits even more.

But be warned: You must be very careful with your translation quality! Always proofread/spell-check your work and run the necessary verification checks in your CAT Tool. Oh, and don't forget to deliver final target files to such clients, since they don't know about CAT Tools and their file formats.

Minimum Charge

Occasionally, you'll receive work that's either too small in volume (i.e., less than 300 words) or requires a quick check on something. In these cases, the rule is to apply a minimum charge to the client. A quick method in calculating this charge based on your word rate, is by multiply 300 with your rate. In this case, the number 300 represents the lowest word count threshold. So the math is as follows:

Word Count Threshold x Word Rate = Minimum Charge

So, if your rate is $0.10, your minimum charge would be:

Word Count Threshold	x	Word Rate	=	Minimum Charge
300	x	$0.10	=	$30

Of course, the above is just a suggested way of figuring out a reasonable minimum charge. You can apply any other method or declare an amount based on your best guess. In any case, please keep it realistic to avoid losing work. And, it's good business practice to skip a few minimum charges if the client is providing a frequent stream of such jobs. This will keep the client happy and throw more work your way.

Indicative Word Rate & Minimum Charge Ranges

To help you get an idea of word rates and minimum charges, I've created the following table for the most popular languages. The numbers appearing in it are not absolute, so you are welcome to adapt to your liking. Note that I've included separate columns of prices for translation agencies and direct customers.

Table - Indicative Pricelist:

Language	For Agency		For Direct Customer	
	From/Into English	Minimum Charge	From/Into English	Minimum Charge
Albanian	$0.05 - $0.08	$15.00 - $22.50	$0.08 - $0.12	$22.50 - $36.00
Arabic	$0.04 - $0.06	$12.00 - $18.00	$0.06 - $0.10	$18.00 - $28.80
Bulgarian	$0.05 - $0.08	$15.00 - $22.50	$0.08 - $0.12	$22.50 - $36.00
Chinese	$0.04 - $0.06	$12.00 - $18.00	$0.06 - $0.10	$18.00 - $28.80
Croatian	$0.05 - $0.08	$15.00 - $22.50	$0.08 - $0.12	$22.50 - $36.00

Language	For Agency		For Direct Customer	
	From/Into English	Minimum Charge	From/Into English	Minimum Charge
Czech	$0.05 - $0.08	$15.00 - $22.50	$0.08 - $0.12	$22.50 - $36.00
Danish	$0.08 - $0.12	$24.00 - $36.00	$0.12 - $0.17	$36.00 - $51.00
Dutch	$0.08 - $0.12	$24.00 - $36.00	$0.12 - $0.17	$36.00 - $51.00
Estonian	$0.05 - $0.08	$15.00 - $22.50	$0.08 - $0.12	$22.50 - $36.00
Finnish	$0.09 - $0.14	$27.00 - $40.50	$0.14 - $0.19	$40.50 - $57.00
French	$0.07 - $0.11	$21.00 - $31.50	$0.11 - $0.16	$31.50 - $48.00
German	$0.07 - $0.11	$21.00 - $31.50	$0.11 - $0.16	$31.50 - $48.00
Greek	$0.05 - $0.08	$15.00 - $22.50	$0.08 - $0.12	$22.50 - $36.00
Hindi	$0.04 - $0.06	$12.00 - $18.00	$0.06 - $0.10	$18.00 - $28.80
Hungarian	$0.05 - $0.08	$15.00 - $22.50	$0.08 - $0.12	$22.50 - $36.00
Italian	$0.06 - $0.09	$18.00 - $27.00	$0.09 - $0.14	$27.00 - $43.20
Japanese	$0.10 - $0.15	$30.00 - $45.00	$0.15 - $0.19	$45.00 - $57.00
Korean	$0.10 - $0.15	$30.00 - $45.00	$0.15 - $0.19	$45.00 - $57.00
Latvian	$0.05 - $0.08	$15.00 - $22.50	$0.08 - $0.12	$22.50 - $36.00
Lithuanian	$0.05 - $0.08	$15.00 - $22.50	$0.08 - $0.12	$22.50 - $36.00
Macedo-nian	$0.05 - $0.08	$15.00 - $22.50	$0.08 - $0.12	$22.50 - $36.00
Norwegian	$0.10 - $0.15	$30.00 - $45.00	$0.15 - $0.19	$45.00 - $57.00
Polish	$0.05 - $0.08	$15.00 - $22.50	$0.08 - $0.12	$22.50 - $36.00
Portu-guese	$0.05 - $0.08	$15.00 - $22.50	$0.08 - $0.12	$22.50 - $36.00

Language	For Agency		For Direct Customer	
	From/Into English	Minimum Charge	From/Into English	Minimum Charge
Romanian	$0.05 - $0.08	$15.00 - $22.50	$0.08 - $0.12	$22.50 - $36.00
Russian	$0.05 - $0.08	$15.00 - $22.50	$0.08 - $0.12	$22.50 - $36.00
Serbian	$0.05 - $0.08	$15.00 - $22.50	$0.08 - $0.12	$22.50 - $36.00
Slovak	$0.05 - $0.08	$15.00 - $22.50	$0.08 - $0.12	$22.50 - $36.00
Slovene	$0.05 - $0.08	$15.00 - $22.50	$0.08 - $0.12	$22.50 - $36.00
Spanish	$0.05 - $0.08	$15.00 - $22.50	$0.08 - $0.12	$22.50 - $36.00
Swedish	$0.08 - $0.12	$24.00 - $36.00	$0.12 - $0.17	$36.00 - $51.00
Turkish	$0.04 - $0.06	$12.00 - $18.00	$0.06 - $0.10	$18.00 - $28.80
Ukrainian	$0.05 - $0.08	$15.00 - $22.50	$0.08 - $0.12	$22.50 - $36.00

You're free to adjust any of the above prices to your requirements, but always keep in mind that you should stay within a logical price range. Anything outside such a range will interfere with your business, causing most probably loss of work.

I'll also give you these two extra web references with which you can further research translation rates:

1. http://search.proz.com/employers/rates
2. http://www.translatorscafe.com/cafe/CommunityRates.asp

Choosing Your CAT Tool

In this line of business, a CAT Tool is your most important implement. I believe Part 2 of this guide made it quite clear. So, how do you choose the best one for your work? The answer isn't as straightforward as it seems, I'm afraid, and depends on various factors such as:

- Budget
- General client requirements
- Computer / Operating System platform
- Technical know-how level
- etc.

If you're just starting out and have a low or non-existent budget, you can pick one of the free CAT Tools out there. The ones I chose to present to you in Part 2 were:

CAT Tool	Link
Heartsome Translation Studio	https://github.com/heartsome/translationstudio8
OmegaT	http://www.omegat.org/

From the two, Heartsome Translation Studio is a safe bet for a free CAT Tool, as its user interface and feature-set resemble more closely those of its proprietary competitors. This means you can transition easily to a more capable (and expensive) CAT Tool once your budget allows it. OmegaT is also another capable free option, but you need to get used to its gawky way of doing things before getting up to speed with it.

If your budget is good enough, then your options are plentiful. But, you need to take into consideration your clients' requirements, especially when dealing with translation agencies. Most often, they define the tool needed for their projects and you need to be aligned to that option. The good thing is that lately, we're seeing a lot of agencies lifting this requirement and allowing translators to use whatever CAT Tool they have. In these cases, they prepare the project files in a format compatible with your tool.

But eventually, you'll start working with agencies that are adamant about using their CAT Tool of choice. The most popular CAT Tools among agencies are:

CAT Tool	Link
SDL Trados Studio	http://www.sdl.com/cxc/language/translation-productivity/trados-studio/
Wordfast	http://www.wordfast.com/
memoQ	https://www.memoq.com/

You won't go wrong picking SDL Trados Studio, since the majority of agencies support it directly or allow receiving files in its format. It's the most pricey of the above three paid CAT Tools, but it's nearly a standard in this industry so you won't go wrong investing in it. Wordfast is a close second, but has seen some recent decline in its use among agencies. It's cheaper than SDL Trados Studio, though, and quite capable as a tool. memoQ is the outsider in this CAT Tool game, but it's managed to place itself as the swiss army knife of all such tools. It supports nearly all other CAT Tool formats, both by importing and exporting them. It also has features not found in any other tool, along with clever implementations of existing features. And, the price is just right for such a tool.

In any case, do your research and make sure to read again section **CAT Tools Panorama!** in Part 2 to get a more detailed overview of these tools. If in doubt, or you're just too new in this business of CAT Tools, try one of the free ones to get up to speed. Once you're confident enough, go pick your tool based on your requirements.

Marketing Your Business (Or How To Find Clients)

One of the toughest things in any profession is finding clients to support your business. The same rule applies to the translation industry, but in this section we'll explore ways to widen your business visibility, making it easier for clients to find you and, at the same time, enable you to locate good project deals.

Creating Or Spicing Up Your Resume/CV

The most basic level of any professional representation is the resume (or CV). Unless you were living under a rock the past few decades, you should know what a resume is, but for clarity's sake I'll remind you: A resume is a brief description of someone's skills in terms of education, qualifications and professional experience.

By definition, a resume is a crucial part of your self-promotional effort. And it's requested by nearly all potential clients so there's no way opting out of it. If you don't have one already then you'll have to bite the bullet and create it with the help provided in this section. If you do have a resume then good for you! But, still, read the suggestions presented here as they will make your resume stand out and increase your possibilities of winning the client.

In the translation industry, resumes are usually reviewed by Vendor Managers. These guys are responsible for finding and evaluating freelancers for their company. Because they deal with hundreds of resumes each day, they apply a specific process that eliminates the bad ones. And by bad I don't mean resumes with irrelevant information. Even if your resume has real and interesting facts, it can be rejected due to wrong presentation order of those facts.

The trick is to provide your information the way a Vendor Manager loves to see it in. So let's find out what that ideal and Vendor Manager-friendly order is for your resume:

1. Begin your resume with your name and contact details. Title this part as **Contact Information**. It should include at least the following:
    - Name:
    - Address:
    - Phone Number:
    - Mobile Number:
    - Email:
    - IM ID (i.e., Skype):
2. Now introduce your mother tongue language and the source and target languages (working pairs) you handle. Title this section as **Working Language Pairs**. You should include the following:
    - Mother Tongue:
    - Source Language(s):

- Target Language(s):

3. Specify your translation services, and title this part as **Translation Services**. These could include:
   - Translation
   - Proofreading
   - Subtitling
   - Transcription
   - Interpreting

4. Indicate your rates for the mentioned working language pairs and translation services. Title this section as **Rates**. An example could be as follows:
   - English => German: $0.10 per word
   - French => German: $0.11 per word
   - Minimum Rate: $25

5. Mention your daily throughput in words. Name this section as **Capacity**. Here's an example on what to include:
   - Translation: 2,500 words/day (excluding/including weekends)
   - Proofreading: 6,500 words/days (excluding/including weekends)

6. Next, you need to outline your specialization fields. Name this part **Specializations**. An example for this section could include:
   - General
   - Technical
   - Medical
   - Life Sciences
   - Finance/Banking
   - Marketing / Advertising
   - etc.

7. Follow with your operating system(s) and software capability. Title this section **Software**. Here's an example:
   - Operating System(s): MS Windows, Mac OS X, Linux
   - Software: MS Office, SDL Trados Studio, Wordfast, memoQ, OmegaT etc.

8. If you have any translation-related work experience, here's the place to insert it, with a title of **Work Experience**. An example could be as follows:
   - 2015 - 2014: Freelance Translator at ACME2 Inc.
   - 2014 - 2013: In-house translator at ACME1 Inc.
   - 2013 - 2012: Pro bono translations for non-profit organization SAVE-BIGFOOT

9. Last, you'll have to place your education background. Name this section **Education** and place all relevant information in it. For example:
   - 2005 - 2001: University of Camelot (Degree / Certification)
   - 2001 - 1997: Institute of Awesome Translators (Degree / Certification)
   - 1997 - 1993: Hogwarts School of Witchcraft and Wizardry (Degree / Certification)

The above nine fields, in the exact order they're presented, will boost your chances of having your resume reviewed by a Vendor Manager. Don't be concerned about any stylistic or cosmetic aspects; even a plain text version will be enough to catch the attention of the person responsible for checking resumes. If you already have a resume then adjust it to the above ordering for maximum impact.

So, to recap, these are the nine fields in the order they need to appear:

1. Contact Information
2. Working Languages Pairs
3. Translation Services
4. Rates
5. Capacity
6. Specializations
7. Software
8. Work Experience
9. Education

Membership-based Translators' Websites

A high-visibility potential for your business can be attained by registering with membership-based websites related to the translation industry. These websites offer free and paid memberships, but you can start with the free service since it covers most of the features we're looking for right now. The benefits of these websites are numerous, so let me outline the most important ones:

- Easy and guided profile creation
- Profile page reachable by search engines (i.e., Google, Bing, Yahoo etc.)
- Access to hundreds of registered translation agencies
- View and get notified of new translation jobs which you can apply to
- Access forums which cover various subjects (technical, terminology etc.)
- View translation agency ratings (also helps you avoid fraudulent agencies)

You can now see why these websites are good for your business. Besides the simple profile creation they offer, in which you're taken by the hand to complete the process, they provide good search engine visibility. This means that when someone searches using your name (or company title) as keywords in Google, Bing, Yahoo or any other search engine, they'll receive in the top results your profile which you've created at these membership-based translators' websites.

This is a big deal. People and companies spend thousands of dollars to make it in the top ranking positions in search results. We're taking a canny shortcut here. We're using the clout of these websites in our favor, since search engines want to see large, nested websites with high traffic and thousands of followers in their social media networks (Facebook, Twitter, YouTube etc.). Quite clever, right?

These websites also offer you easy access to translation agencies which have registered themselves there too. This, in consequence, allows you to view their job postings and gives you the ability to apply to any suitable job offering. Plus, and this is very crucial as we'll see later on, you can view a translation agency's track history, which effectively means that you can see how other translators have rated these companies. This will allow you to stay clear of scammer agencies.

As of this writing, the four most prominent membership-based translators' websites are the following:

Membership-based Website	Link
Proz.com	http://www.proz.com
Translatorscafe.com	http://www.translatorscafe.com
TranslationDirectory.com	http://www.translationdirectory.com
Aquarius	http://www.aquarius.net

I'd strongly suggest you sign-up to all of them or, at a bare minimum, to the first two (Proz.com & Translatorscafe.com). Once you get up to speed with your business it's worth revisiting these websites to see whether you should upgrade your membership to the paid versions. In most cases, the paid subscriptions offer additional benefits that can boost your work potential, so it's worth the investment.

Note: Be sure to also check out **Appendix 3: List of Translation Companies** in which I've included a hundred or so translation agencies that are worth contacting. I've checked them out one-by-one and have provided you with the right contact details (email or web form address) required to apply to. So, take advantage of this list!

Social Networks: LinkedIn, Facebook, Twitter, Google+

You should've guessed this coming. Social networks are the new black, as the saying goes. And it's about time we used their gossipy foundations for our purposes. As with membership-based websites, we can take advantage of their vast internet presence and influence on search engines. The most popular social networks worth using for our cause are:

- LinkedIn
- Facebook
- Twitter
- Google+

LinkedIn can be considered the Facebook of the business world. It's the world's largest online professional network with a mission to connect professionals and make them productive and successful. So, you clearly need to register (it's free) with LinkedIn and start making some useful connections. Make sure you identify your translation profession correctly while creating your profile; this is crucial since LinkedIn will provide information and suggested connections based on your profession. Once registered, start sending connection requests to people in the translation industry and join some translation-related groups. You'll also get access to thousands of job postings (in-house or freelance translation work) from the largest translation agencies and well-known direct customers.

Facebook doesn't need any introductions. Everyone knows about it and everyone uses it (albeit for the wrong reasons). Most probably you already have a Facebook account so you're set to go (if you don't, you know the drill). Once you're set up, you need to mention your translation activity on your profile page, and start following some translation-related groups. The idea is to make a buzz among your Facebook friends of you being a translator now, and starting that avalanche mode for which Facebook is so good at.

You might be wondering why Twitter is in this list. Well, for starters, it will give you internet visibility thanks to how search engines work. Second, everyone has a Twitter account even if they don't know exactly what it is or how to properly use it. Plus, you never know when one of your tweets becomes viral, thrusting you to a whole new popularity level!

As for Google+, there's not much to say other than it's Google's attempt of a direct hit on Facebook. So, yes, it's another social network that tries to connect you with your friends and your friends' friends and share all kinds of questionable information. The only reason I'm suggesting you register with this network is because Google is behind it, automatically meaning that you'll have another extra layer of search engine visibility. Remember, companies pay thousands of dollars for such visibility, so don't take it lightly when you have free options for it.

Online Business Directories

Another way for locating potential clients is by checking out online business directories. These websites are like your typical yellow pages but with many more options in terms of searchability: You can apply search filters that can narrow down your results to the finest detail. The real benefit of looking into such business directories is the discovery of direct customers (i.e., non-agencies), who as we've stated yield considerably better profits. But, be warned, such a process isn't at all easy and doesn't always guarantee positive results. On the other hand, if you do succeed in luring in a direct customer, you'll be making some very good money.

First of all, we don't want you going on a wild goose chase, so we need to define some criteria here on which you can base your search on. I've done the background research for you and can thus present you with the types of companies you should pursue on these online business directories. The following business categories offer the most potential at establishing a collaboration channel with them:

- **Companies in the subject field you cover:** This is a bit obvious, but regularly overlooked. So, if your main subject field is consumer electronics, you should set your search filter to begin with such types of businesses. There's no reason selecting all types of companies and going through the search results when you can only translate for specific subject fields. This will significantly narrow down your results, allowing you to focus more quickly on the interesting companies.

- **Multinational companies:** By having offices in more than one country, these companies give you a better chance of landing a translation job. You should seek out such multinational businesses that match your language pair(s). Don't limit your search only to the head office or headquarters of such companies. Make sure to approach their overseas branch offices as well.

- **Import/Export companies:** The trading business has great potential for translation jobs. Look for any such company that imports or exports stuff around the globe. Most likely, they will need help with translating documentation regarding their imported/exported products.

- **Manufacturers:** In contrast to import/export companies, manufacturers fabricate their own products. In other words, manufacturers produce the stuff that import/export companies push around the world. So, this is like going right to the source, which is a good thing to do, since these companies are usually faced with the burden of providing their products with translated documentation (i.e., manuals, certificates and so on). Just make sure to check their website to find out whether your language pair suits them.

- **Software companies:** This is a special case that deserves inclusion in your search opportunities. Software developing houses always seek ways to expand their user base, and the easiest way to do this is by offering localized (a.k.a. translated) versions of their software. If you include here the mobile apps market and the various online platforms you quickly get an idea of how huge this market is. So make sure to look for such companies.

A good practice when searching for any type of client is having a common reference point where all useful information is gathered into for further action or later assessment. For example, you could create a spreadsheet file in MS Excel (or any other spreadsheet software you prefer) which would include the details of these potential clients, along with information regarding your contacting process. It could look something like this:

Company Name	Phone Number	Contact Email/Link	Contact Date	Result	Follow-Up Date	Notes
ACME1 Inc.	555-0199	info@acme1.com	5/27/15	No response	6/27/15	Call them?
ACME2 Inc.	555-0110	www.acme2.com/contact-form/	4/12/15	Will notify me once they have something suitable	5/12/15	Contact Joe Doe directly at jdoe@acme2.com
ACME3 Inc.	555-0134	contact@acme3.com	3/8/15	Added me in their vendor database	4/8/15	As contact details of German branch office

Online Business Directory Contact List

This way you'll stay organized and focused to the process, allowing you to better manage the procedure once the list starts getting bigger. Of course, you're free to add any other information you deem important in such a list. Mine is just an example to get you started.

And now let me list some of the interesting online business directories with which you can begin your client hunt:

Business Directory Name	Link
Kompass	http://www.kompass.com
Yellow Pages (YP)	http://www.yellowpages.com
BizBilla.com	http://www.bizbilla.com
go4WorldBusiness.com	http://www.go4worldbusiness.com/
Alibaba	http://www.alibaba.com
EUROPAGES	http://www.europages.com
ECVV	http://www.ecvv.com
Allactiontrade	http://www.allactiontrade.com

Your Personal Website

Although optional, a personal website that is dedicated to your translation service will add up to your internet visibility and look good on your business card too. Plus, it gives you a more professional appeal and distinguishes you from the rest, something that clients will certainly take note of.

Your options of having a website depend on your technical know-how or lack thereof. What I mean is that you can either create it yourself if you have the knowledge of doing so, or pay someone else to create it for you. If you have some basic computer knowledge then I can suggest the following website creation software that ease the process considerably:

Website Creation Tool	Operating System	Link
RapidWeaver	Mac OS X	https://realmacsoftware.com/rapidweaver/
Freeway Pro	Mac OS X	http://www.softpress.com/freeway-pro/
Sandvox	Mac OS X	http://www.karelia.com/products/sandvox/
Artisteer	MS Windows	http://www.artisteer.com/
Xara Web Designer	MS Windows	http://www.xara.com/eu/web-designer/
WebSite X5	MS Windows	http://www.websitex5.com
WebPlus X8	MS Windows	http://www.serif.com/webplus

The above website creation tools are quite straightforward and allow you to select from several pre-built templates cutting in half the creation time. Note, though, that if you choose to do it alone, you'll need to buy your own domain name and hosting plan. The first represents your web address and the latter is the space at which you're site will be uploaded to, enabling it to be viewed by anyone on the internet. On the other hand, if you're not up to the challenge you could look around for some cheap solutions and have it done by a professional.

At a bare minimum your website should include the following pages:

- **Home Page:** Also called an intro page, this is the first thing your visitor sees once getting to your website. On this page you need to include a short introduction about yourself and your translation services.
- **Services Page:** Here you will provide a detailed description of your translation services such as working language pair(s), type of service (i.e., translation, proofreading, subtitling, interpreting), word rates and minimum charges, daily throughput and anything else you think a client needs to know about.
- **About Me Page:** On this page you should say a few words about yourself. Keep it professional and mention anything that has to do about you and your translation practice.
- **Contact Page:** Here you'll include your contact details such as address, phone/fax number, email and so on. Have in mind that, instead of showing your email on this page (which can lead to a lot of spam in your mailbox), you could create a web form that will protect your email and send the form's submitted information to you instantly.

Pro Bono Service

One more way to find clients and, at the same time, sharpen your translation skills and experience, is by offering pro bono translation help. This means that you'll be working for free, but your name will be circulating around catching the attention of some potential clients. There's no need or obligation to translate anything huge in volume. Most often, this free help concerns small batches of documents and you can usually pick which parts you think are manageable.

These pro bono translation services will also give a boost to your resume, filling it up nicely. And, most importantly, you'll feel good with yourself by offering much needed help to different causes. So, check out the list below which contains organizations seeking volunteer translators and give them a hand:

- http://www.onlinevolunteers.org
- http://www.kidlink.org
- http://www.micahnetwork.org
- http://www.babels.org
- http://www.idealist.org
- http://www.unitedplanet.org

Organizing Your Work

A very important aspect of any freelance work is organizing it in the most simple yet effective way. Even if you already apply some type of arrangement scheme and think it does the job good enough, I strongly urge you to keep reading this section and learn about my way of sorting out things. I'm sure you'll find some interest bits to incorporate into your own workflow model.

Project Dashboard

Let's start with my favorite one, the Project Dashboard. Despite the pompous name, it's just a simple but very effective way to see what's going on with your translation projects. The idea is based on having a central location with all vital project data and metrics. And the good part is that you can easily accomplish this by using any type of spreadsheet software.

To keep things as simple as possible, here's a bare minimum project dashboard example:

Status	Deadline	Client	PO #	Service	Project Name	Quantity	Price	Tax/Vat	Amount	Currency	Notes
In Progress	7/24/15	ACME1 Inc.	4321-AB	Translation (EN => DE)	Ad Brochure	1200	0.10	0	120	USD	
Completed	6/21/15	ACME2 Inc.	9876-CD	Translation (FR => DE)	Coffee Maker Manual	500	0.11	0	55	EUR	
Invoiced	5/14/15	ACME3 Inc.	EF-5678	Proofreading (DE)	Automotive Document	2	25	0	50	USD	Invoice #23
On Hold	4/18/15	ACME4 Inc.	TR-09172	Translation (DE => EN)	Marketing Memo	1	250	0	250	EUR	Client to update material
Canceled	3/16/15	ACME5 Inc.	REV-3989	Translation (DE => FR)	Financial Report	2500	0.12	0	300	USD	

Project Dashboard Example

Now, let me quickly describe the logic behind each column so you can see how easy and useful this proves to be:

- **Status** column: Here you should include the state (or condition) of a project. This way, with a just a glance you can find out what's happening with your projects. I suggest you include and use at least the following fields and stick to them as much as possible:
  - **In Progress**: Used when a project is being worked on.
  - **Completed**: Used for a project that has been finished but not invoiced yet.
  - **Invoiced**: Used for a project that has been completed and invoiced.
  - **On Hold**: Used for a project that has been temporarily postponed.
  - **Cancelled**: Used for a project that has been called off.
- **Deadline** column: In this column you should insert a project's deadline that has been agreed with the client. Depending on your spreadsheet software, you can enable an auto-coloring feature which will color a deadline to a particular color (i.e., red) when reaching a specific date. This is a good visual cue that will grab your attention when mostly needed (**Note:** You can also apply this auto-coloring to other columns, for example to the Status column, allowing for a much better visual understanding of your dashboard).
- **Client** column: Here you'll insert your client's name.

- **PO #** column: This is where you include the Purchase Order number a client provides you with when assigning you a project. It's very important to note this down here as you're usually forced to include it in your invoice, once a job is completed. If a client doesn't provide PO numbers you can just insert "N/A" in this column which stands for "Not Available".

- **Service** column: In this column you'll be inserting the service type (i.e., translation, proofreading etc.) and language pair involved for a project. I suggest you follow the style in the table above which is **Service (Source Language => Target Language)**.

- **Project Name** column: Include here the project's name or code. Don't be creative, just stick to the project name or assignment number your client has provided you with. This is crucial so you retain a consistent reference point with the client.

- **Quantity** column: This is where you'll insert the word count or hours of a project. Since we only have a single field in this column, you need to be careful when dealing with word counts. If the client has provided a weighted word count then you're okay and simply need to insert it here. If you've only received an analysis log (a.k.a. TM Match log) then you either can calculate the weighted words yourself as shown in Part 2 under section **Word Counts, The Trados Discount Model & Weighted Words**, or insert "1" here and add the total job cost in the next column, titled **Price**, so the total amount in column **Amount** is, correctly, the total cost of the job.

- **Price** column: Here you'll insert your word rate or minimum/hourly charge, depending on the project requirements.

- **Tax/Vat** column: If you have any service Tax or Vat requirements in your state or country, this is the place to add it. Make sure to check whether you're free of these, which is usually the case when freelancing for foreign companies. Check with an accountant if in doubt. If you're required to add a Tax or Vat rate, then you'll need to apply a formula in this column to calculate the values based on the data in column **Amount**. This formula (which is a simple calculation) should be provided by an accountant who knows the requirements for your case. For simplicity's sake, or if you're not obliged by any such things, just add a "0" in this cell.

- **Amount** column: This is where the total project cost is calculated. In its simple form, it will multiply the values in **Quantity** with the values in **Price**. So, you should insert the corresponding formula in the cells of this column. You can do this by double-clicking on the cell and typing "=[Quantity]*[Price]" (without the quotes), where **[Quantity]** and **[Price]** should be replaced by the actual cell codes for those columns. Look at this screenshot to understand what I mean:

H	I	J	K	L
Quantity	Price	Tax/Vat	Amount	Currency
1200	0.10	0	=H2*I2	USD
500	0.11	0	55	EUR
2	25	0	50	USD
1	250	0	250	EUR
2500	0.12	0	300	USD

Amount Calculation

So, in this case the cell code for **[Quantity]** is **H2** and for **[Price]** it's **I2**.

If you're required to include any Tax or Vat numbers, then this calculation gets a bit more interesting. Again, you need an accountant's input on this and he/she will easily provide you with the corresponding calculation formula for you to insert in this cell.

- **Currency** column: The only reason I'm including such a column here is because you might come across a client that can only pay in a different currency than yours. This isn't very common nowadays, but you never know what the future has in store for you. In any case, you're free to remove this column if you don't like receiving money in foreign currencies.

- **Notes** column: You can insert here anything related to your project, like follow-up notes, reminders, invoice numbers and so on. Look at it as your personal scratchpad.

I think the benefits of using a Project Dashboard are quite clear, especially now that you've seen the concept behind it. You'll be thankful too, once you start dabbling with more than one project a time! So, try it out or adjust your current workflow model to it.

Tree Folder Structure

Keeping an eye on your projects is one thing. Storing them properly on your computer is another. And believe me when I say that things can get out of control quickly, once project files start piling up. You need an easy way of categorizing your projects and keeping them in a logical structure on your computer. This will cut down tracking times, ease the management of any project, and allow effortless back-ups.

The project file storing method I'll be showing you is called the **Tree Folder Structure**, and is based on the idea of tiers, which is basically layers of stuff stacked in a clear and coherent way. You won't be needing any special software other than the typical file manager that comes with your operating system (i.e., Windows Explorer for MS Windows, Finder for Mac OS X).

First, you'll need to pick a suitable location on your computer to store the master folder (a.k.a. top tree-level folder, or root folder), which will include all other relevant subfolders. Any location will do, but be sure to select a place that's easy to access since you'll be going there a lot. For example, you could select the **My Documents** folder in MS Windows, or the **Documents** folder is Mac OS X.

Once you've picked the right spot, create a folder with the name **Projects**. Under this folder you'll be creating various subfolders with specific naming conventions to host the project files. To make this as clear as possible, I'll show you how this works by including and describing the below screenshot:

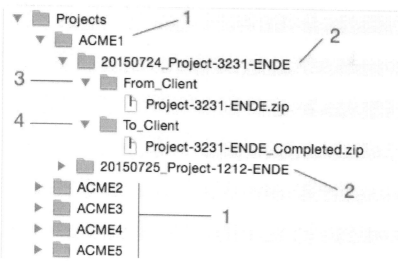

Tree Folder Structure

In the above image you can see that we've created separate folders for each client (1). If we look into one of these client folders, we'll see that for each project we've created a corresponding subfolder (2) and gave it a name that follows the convention **[Start Date]_[Project Name]-[SourceTarget Language]**. So the first project folder we see under client ACME1 is **20150724_Project-3231-ENDE**, which breaks down into the following information:

- Start Date: July 24th, 2015
- Project Name: Project 3231
- Source & Target Language: ENDE (EN = English, DE = German)
  - **Note:** The 2-letter naming convention you see here (EN and DE) is that of ISO 639-1, a standardized nomenclature used to classify languages. You can check a table of all know languages under the 2-letter and 3-letter ISO codes in **Appendix 2: ISO Language Codes**.

Inside the project folder you'll find two more folders, one named **From_Client** (3) and the other **To_Client** (4). As their names hint, here is where you'll place the files received from a client (3) and, once you've translated them, the place to store them before sending back (4).

This whole tree folder structure and naming scheme will allow you to work a lot more efficiently, keeping things tidy and well organized. Once you get used to it, you'll be wondering how you'd been working without it all this time! And, here's an extra little secret: This process is also compatible with ISO 9001 procedures so you'll be applying a process that a lot of companies pay good bucks to learn and implement in their workflow.

A Word About Purchase Orders & Invoices

This is a good spot to briefly talk about purchase orders (POs) and invoices. The reason I'm doing this is because I've seen a lot of translators, even experienced ones, either confusing the two terms, not requesting POs, or not preparing correctly their invoices. It's in your own interest to make sure you handle properly these cases. Clients frequently issue wrong POs or reject invoices that don't follow their invoicing rules. At the end of the day, it's your money in jeopardy here, so there's no reason to treat these things lightly.

So let's start with purchase orders, or POs as they are most commonly referred as in the translation industry. A PO, which is issued by clients, is a document that includes some key information regarding a service assigned to you (i.e., a translation project) such as project name, volume, cost, deadline and so on, along with other vital details that will be needed when you'll be invoicing this project. The first thing to do when you're assigned a project is to request a PO. If the work is coming from a translation agency then they're obligated to send you a PO, so be assertive with them if they delay this task. If the client isn't an agency, then it depends on their company policy whether they can issue a PO or not. In this case, you can kindly request one but don't push too much if they cannot provide it. Once you receive a PO, you must always check it to make sure the information is correct. Make sure the rate and deadline are the ones agreed upon, and read any small print in there, usually at the end of the document, to avoid any payment policy tricks. It's important you do this the moment the PO is received and before starting any work. This way you'll avoid any nasty surprises that might be lurking around after delivering your work.

On the other hand, invoices are documents you have to pre-pare and send to the client. An invoice needs to include information found in a client's PO, such as PO number, total cost mentioned in PO and so on. If no PO was provided then you need to include some details that can define the project you were assigned, like project name or code, project start date, project cost. Your invoice must also clearly state your pre-ferred method of payment along with any required details. For example, if you prefer to be paid by bank wire then you need to provide your bank account number (or IBAN number if applicable), your bank's name, SWIFT or BIC code (if appli-cable), and beneficiary name. If you prefer PayPal, then simply mention it and indicate your PayPal ID. Always check the client's payment policy (i.e., 30-day payment after receiv-ing invoice, 45-day payment after project completion etc.) and note it in your invoice too.

Moreover, the Project Dashboard we described earlier on can prove quite handy for keeping track of POs and invoices. By looking at it you can instantly see whether you have received a PO or not, and verify if you've invoiced a specific project. So, be vigilant when dealing with POs and invoices. After all, it's your money we're talking about!

Backups! Backups! Backups!

Yes, backups. I can't stress this out as much as I'd like to, but setting up some kind of backup process should be a top pri-ority for your business. If you don't have the cash to buy a dedicated backup software for your platform, then don't fret. There are free solutions and methods by using only the soft-ware that comes with your operating system. For simplicity's sake, I'll outline a free and easy method that can be applied to all platforms.

The software tools you'll need for this simple backup process are already included in your operating system. The only extra thing you should have or need to purchase is a USB flash drive or an external USB hard disk. So, here's how this simple backup process works:

1. Locate your main working folder in which all client project files are located, along with the completed files you deliver back to them. If you're using our Tree Folder Structure process, you should have everything under the folder **Projects**. Right-click on this top-level folder and select from the context menu the corresponding option for compressing the folder:

Mac OS X context menu:

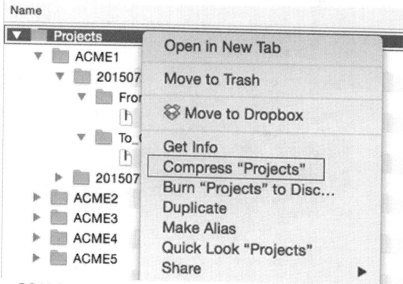

OS X Compress Folder

MS Windows context menu:

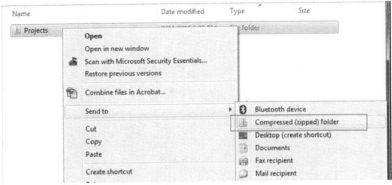

MS Win Compress Folder

2. Depending on your operating system you may or may not be asked first for a name for this compressed file. In any case, the naming convention I suggest using for such backups is this one:

[BackupDate]-[FolderName]-Backup.zip

An actual example is as follows:

20150725-Projects-Backup.zip

The date convention I'm using here is YYYYMMDD (YYYY = Year, MM = Month, DD = Day), so 20150725 is July 25th, 2015. This date convention will give you a nice sorting order when you start pilling up backup files, allowing you to quickly locate a specific backup when required.

3. Once you complete the above steps, you'll end up with a zip file that contains your backup. Now connect your external USB flash drive or USB hard disk and open up its contents in your file manager. Create a new folder with the name **Project-Backups** and move your backup zip file in there. This will be the place where you'll be storing all future backups.

We're using an external storage device for our backups for two important reasons:

1. You should always keep at least one extra copy of your important files.
2. The extra copy should always reside on an external storage device and never at the same location with your original files.

Point 1 is obvious, since that's the primary function of taking backups. As for point 2, the reason we need backups to reside on an external storage device is to avoid any corruption of the disk on which the original files and their backups reside on, in which case you lose all files. It's pure logic. Plus, an external storage device is portable so you can take it with you or store it at a remote location for extra security.

Now regarding the frequency of creating these backups, I'd suggest anything from bi-weekly to monthly, depending on the amount of work you're handling. Of course, you're free to do a quicker cycle if that will make you sleep better.

Note: There are other free backup solutions available on Mac OS X and MS Windows, but these vary and depend on the version of the operating system. For example, on Mac OS X, there's Time Machine (https://support.apple.com/en-us/HT201250) which features an easy set up and process for backing up your files. On MS Windows things are more tricky because different backup methods are available based on operating system version. So, for example, on MS Windows 7 you have Backup and Restore (http://windows.microsoft.com/en-us/windows/back-up-files#1TC=windows-7), while on MS Windows 8 (and MS Windows 10) there's the File History (http://windows.microsoft.com/en-us/windows-8/what-happened-to-backup-restore) feature.

Last, when working with any type of software such as a CAT Tool or an office suite application like a word processor or spreadsheet program, always make sure to save frequently. Usually, the keyboard shortcut for such a function is Ctrl+S for MS Windows and GNU/Linux systems and CMD+S for Mac OS X. Make it a habit, otherwise you'll surely regret it one day.

Client Relationship Quick Tips

I think it would be useful here to give you some extra pointers regarding proper client interaction. These ten quick tips are based on my experience as a Translation and Localization Project Manager, and regard the issues I encountered while collaborating with freelance translators. This is another "inside" advice topic, so you should pay close attention to the information I'll be providing below. By taking note and following this advice you'll secure a healthy client relationship, which will lead to a steady and increasing workflow. The following tips don't follow any particular order, though I've tried to sort them out based on a rough chronological order:

1. **Always clarify client's payment policy:** Before you start any translation work for a new client you should always ask them about their company payment policy. Don't confuse this with your word rate, which you should agree upon when dealing with translation projects. A company's payment policy refers to how and when you get paid. More specifically, you should ask them about these three things:

    - Payment time-frame
    - Invoicing process
    - Payment methods

The payment time-frame deals with the amount of time between your completed job and your payment. It could be anything from instant payment upon delivery, to 30-60 days after delivery. Every company has its own payment time-frame so be sure to clarify it.

Invoicing also differs among clients. That's why you need to ask then about their invoicing process. Most companies require you send them one while others allow you to do the invoicing on their website, using a special intranet platform. Also, some clients require invoices to be prepared in a specific way, with particular information obtained from their PO. So check with them.

As for payment methods, this is quite important information, since clients are able to use various payment methods such as PayPal, Skrill (ex Moneybookers), Western Union, bank deposit (a.k.a. wire transfer), bank check and so on. So you see the reasons behind this question of making clear your payment method.

2. **Respect NDAs / Read them carefully before signing:** NDA stands for Non-Disclosure Agreement, and is a binding contract between you and a client that outlines how you should deal with confidential material, knowledge, or information. In simple English, it's a document with various gagging clauses forbidding you from publicly disclosing any information regarding a specific translation project. Someday you'll come across such a project and will need to sign an NDA to get the job done. That's why you need to read it carefully and make sure that all clauses are reasonable and compatible with your line of work.

3. **Don't take more than you can handle:** Such a simple rule, but you can't imagine how often translators take more than they can handle causing havoc everywhere. So don't be generous and request only the volume you can safely handle, even when the client is pushing you to take more.

4. **Don't handle subject fields you're not comfortable with:** Like point 3 above, this is another simple rule to follow. So don't mess it up! Translate only subject fields you know about.

5. **Always request a PO:** If the client is a translation agency then they will always provide you with a Purchase Order. Request it at the beginning of the project so you can make sure it contains the correct information (rates, deadline etc.) since you'll be using this data for your invoice later on. If you're dealing with direct customers (non-agencies) they might not have a PO issuing system in use, so in this case use the information in your email exchange with the direct customer which should include rates, deadline etc. and can be used as a PO substitute.

6. **Follow client's/project's instructions carefully:** As straightforward as this seems, you can't imagine how many translators fail to do it. Don't be one of them. Read and re-read the instructions as many times as needed, and revisit them again if in doubt, especially before delivering back to the client.

7. **Be reachable (phone, text message, email, IM):** We're not talking about 24/7 availability, but you need to be reachable during most of the client's working ours. For example, things may change for a project you're handling or maybe the client needs immediate information about something concerning the work you're doing. It's helpful to provide clients with more ways of contacting you other than email, so feel free to give them a phone number or IM id (i.e., Skype).

8. **Be frank when problems occur:** Trust me when I say that you'll do more damage to your reputation when not admitting you have a severe problem with your work, the moment such a bad thing occurs. And the more time you let go by without mentioning the problem the more damage you're causing to the client. So stand up to the task and let the client know immediately about the issues you're having before it's too late!

9. **Don't go MIA:** MIA stands for Missing In Action. And that means you shouldn't pull a Houdini to a client for whatever reasons. If you've been assigned work then you should finish the job as instructed. If, for any reason, something changes in the process that doesn't allow you to complete the assignment then you must inform the client in a timely manner. Failing to do so will blacklist you from the client's Vendor Team, and could lead to further repercussions for your professional translation career. So be a professional and don't go MIA.

10. **Invoice correctly:** Just a reminder again that you should invoice based on a client's invoicing policies. As stated in point 1, you should ask the client to outline their invoicing process and you need to make sure you follow it correctly to avoid any delays with your payment.

Avoiding Fraudulent Clients

Scammers can be found everywhere, and the translation industry is no exception to the rule. I'm afraid there's no easy way of exposing them, but with the help of some suggestions that I'll be outlining here you should be able to steer clear from such frauds. I'll be showing you three simple check methods that usually don't take much time to carry out and, by combining all three, will give you the best possible hint on whether you're dealing with a scammer or not.

1. **Checking forum pages of membership-based translators' websites:** The best place to check first is the forum pages of the various membership-based translators' websites. As we mentioned earlier on, these websites offer forums that mention and rate translation agencies around the world. You can use the available forum search box and find out whether your new client is okay or not. Go back to section **Membership-based Translators' Websites** to get the list with these useful sites. Worth mentioning here is Proz.com's Blue Board (http://www.proz.com) which is a searchable database of translation agencies with feedback from fellow translators.

2. **Using search engines with specific keywords:** In today's internet era anything's possible with a search engine. So, by using specific keywords you can obtain some quite interesting results. For example, a simple but very effective keyword search could be:

   [ClientName] payment

   Where [ClientName], obviously, is the name of the client you're trying to do a background check on. For example:

ACME payment

You could use any other suitable keyword as well, as long as it follows the client's name in the search engine's text box. So fire up your search engine of choice (Google, Bing, Yahoo etc.) and start the detective work!

3. **Client contact details verification:** Sometimes, you need to be sure that who's talking to you is actually who he/she says he/she is. This is also true for a company's name and address, which you need to be able to verify as well. Again, the search engine is your friend, so type in the client or company name you have and see what comes up. An extra, impressive step would be to use Google Maps (https://www.google.com/maps) and its Street View mode which will allow you to see the physical location of the building in which your client has his/her office!

So keep your eyes wide open and do your background research when negotiating work with new clients.

Appendix 1: Translation Industry Glossary

Term	Description
100% Match	A translated segment that already exists in a TM.
Across	A proprietary CAT Tool from Across Systems GmbH (http://www.my-across.net/en/index.aspx).
Alignment	The process of matching source and target segments for the creation of a TM.
ASAP	Abbreviation for **As Soon As Possible.**
Back Translation	The process of translating a document from its target language back into its source language. This allows for better quality checks on the translation.
Bilingual File	(a.k.a. Unclean File) - A file that contains both the source text and the target translation. Usually refers to CAT Tool files.
CAT Tool	Abbreviation for **C**omputer-**A**ssisted **T**ranslation Tool. A CAT Tool is a specialized computer program that aids the translator during translation activities.
Certified Translation	A translation that has been done or reviewed by a sworn translator. This translation can be used for legal purposes.
Clean File	(a.k.a. Target File) - A file that contains only the target language translation and follows the source file's format and layout.
Close Of Business	Indicates a specific time-frame that coincides with business closing hours.
COB	Abbreviation for **C**lose **O**f **B**usiness. Indicates a specific time-frame that coincides with business closing hours.
Computer-Assisted Translation Tool	(a.k.a. CAT Tool) - A Computer-Assisted Translation Tool is a specialized computer program that aids the translator during translation activities.

Term	Description
Concordance	The process of searching within a TM for the existing translations of a specific word or phrase.
Consistency	The process of checking whether a segment has been translated the same way.
Context Match	(a.k.a. ICE Match, Perfect Match) - A segment that has at least a 100% Match in the TM and the preceding segment is identical in both the TM and document.
Country Code	A two or three letter code with a standardized nomenclature used to classify country names.
Déjà Vu	A proprietary CAT Tool from Atril (http://www.atril.com).
Desktop Publishing	(a.k.a. DTP) - The process of preparing documentation (format and layout) for publication (print or online).
DNT	Abbreviation for Do Not Translate.
Do Not Translate	a.k.a. DNT.
DOC	Microsoft Word file format.
DOCX	Microsoft Word file format.
DTP	Desktop Publishing is the process of preparing documentation (format & layout) for publication (print or online).
End Of Business	Indicates a specific time-frame that coincides with business closing hours.
EOB	Abbreviation for End Of Business. Indicates a specific time-frame that coincides with business closing hours.
FIGS	Abbreviation for French, Italian, German and Spanish.
Fluency	A proprietary CAT Tool from Western Standard (https://www.westernstandard.com).
Fuzzy Match	A TM segment that is partially similar to the current segment being translated.

Term	Description
G11N	Abbreviation for Globalization. The number 11 represents the eleven characters that are between the first letter, G, and the last letter, N. Globalization is the process of adapting services or products to the global market.
Globalization	(a.k.a. G11N) - The process of adapting services or products to the global market.
Glossary	A list of specific domain terms with their definitions. A bilingual glossary contains the terms and definitions in both source and target languages.
Heartsome Translation Studio	A free CAT Tool (was proprietary) from Heartsome (https://github.com/heartsome/translationstudio8).
Hourly Rate	The cost of a service based on a per hour charge.
HTML	Abbreviation for HyperText Markup Language. HTML is a markup language for creating web pages.
I18N	Abbreviation for Internationalization. The number 18 represents the eighteen characters that are between the first letter, I, and the last letter, N. Internationalization is the process of designing a product from the ground-up with support for easy language adaptation (localization).
ICE Match	(a.k.a. Context Match, Perfect Match) - ICE stands for In Context Exact. An ICE Match is a segment that has at least a 100% Match in the TM and the preceding segment is identical in both the TM and document.
IDML	Abbreviation for InDesign Markup Language. An Adobe InDesign file format.
In-Country Review	The reviewing a translation by a native person of the target language who resides in the country where the text will be used.

Term	Description
Internationalization	(a.k.a. I18N) - The process of designing a product from the ground-up with support for easy language adaptation (localization).
INX	Abbreviation for InDesign Interchange File. An Adobe InDesign file format.
ITD	SDLX bilingual file format.
L10N	Abbreviation for Localization. The number 10 represents the ten characters that are between the first letter, L, and the last letter, N. Localization is the process of adapting services or products to a specific locale.
Language Code	A two or three letter code with a standardized nomenclature used to classify language names.
Language Pair	The working languages that a translator works with.
Language Quality Assurance	(a.k.a. LQA, QA) - The process that checks translation quality and provides procedures to identify translation quality errors.
Language Service Provider	(a.k.a. LSP) - A company that provides language services, such as translation, localization, interpretation etc.
Language Sign-Off	(a.k.a. LSO) - The process of finalizing a translation that has passed LQA.
Leverage	The process of assessing and re-using previous translations in a new project.
LISA	Abbreviation for Localization Industry Standards Association.
Localization	(a.k.a. L10N) - The process of adapting services or products to a specific locale.
LQA	Abbreviation for Language Quality Assurance. The process that checks translation quality and provides procedures to identify translation quality errors.
LSO	The process of finalizing a translation that has passed LQA.

Term	Description
LSP	Abbreviation for **L**anguage **S**ervice **P**rovider. A company that provides language services, such as translation, localization, interpretation etc.
Machine Translation	(a.k.a. MT) - The use of a computer software or platform to translate text without any human interaction. Do not confuse with CAT Tools.
memoQ	A proprietary CAT Tool from Kilgray (https://www.memoq.com).
Memsource	A proprietary CAT Tool from Memsource (https://www.memsource.com).
MIF	Abbreviation for **M**aker **I**nterchange **F**ormat. MIF is an Adobe FrameMaker file format.
Minimum Charge	The lowest amount applicable to an offered service.
MLV	Abbreviation for **M**ulti-**L**anguage **V**endor. A company that provides multi-language services, such as translation, localization, interpretation etc.
MQXLIFF	memoQ bilingual file format.
MT	The use of a computer software or platform to translate text without any human interaction. Do not confuse with CAT Tools.
Multi-Language Vendor	(a.k.a. MLV) - A company that provides multi-language services, such as translation, localization, interpretation etc.
NDA	Abbreviation for **N**on-**D**isclosure **A**greement. An NDA is a binding contract between two parties that outlines how these parties should deal with confidential material, knowledge, or information.
No Match	A segment that has no TM matches.
Non-Disclosure Agreement	(a.k.a. NDA) - A binding contract between two parties that outlines how these parties should deal with confidential material, knowledge, or information.
ODP	LibreOffice/OpenOffice file format.

Term	Description
ODS	LibreOffice/OpenOffice file format.
ODT	LibreOffice/OpenOffice file format.
Office Suite	A bundle of productivity software such as a Word Processor, a Spreadsheet Program, a Presentation Program etc. Examples of Office Suites are Microsoft Office and LibreOffice.
OmegaT	A free CAT Tool from open source team OmegaT (http://www.omegat.org).
Page Rate	The cost of a service based on a per page charge.
PDF	Abbreviation for **P**ortable **D**ocument **F**ormat. An Adobe Acrobat file format.
Perfect Match	(a.k.a. ICE Match, Context Match) - A segment that has at least a 100% Match in the TM and the preceding segment is identical in both the TM and document.
PM	Abbreviation for **P**roject **M**anager. The person responsible for planning, executing and completing a project.
PO	Abbreviation for **P**urchase **O**rder. A document that indicates type, quantity, and agreed price for products or services.
POT	Abbreviation for **P**ortable **O**bject **T**ype. A file format that contains software strings for translation in any text editor.
PPT	Microsoft PowerPoint file format.
PPTX	Microsoft PowerPoint file format.
PPW	(a.k.a. Word Rate) - Abbreviation for **P**rice **P**er **W**ord. The cost of a service based on a per word charge.
Pre-Translation	The process of passing files through a TM for automatic insertion of existing translations.
Price Per Word	The cost of a service based on a per word charge.
Project Manager	The person responsible for planning, executing and completing a project.
Proofreading	The process of checking a translation in terms of spelling, grammar and syntax.

Term	Description
Pseudo-Translation	The process of simulating a completed translation process, allowing evaluation of the resulting target documents to uncover hidden costs or bottle-necks.
Purchase Order	(a.k.a. PO) - A document that indicates type, quantity, and agreed price for products or services.
QA	Abbreviation for **Q**uality **A**ssurance. The process that checks translation quality and provides procedures to identify translation quality errors.
Quality Assurance	(a.k.a. QA, LQA) - The process that checks translation quality and provides procedures to identify translation quality errors.
Repetition Match	An identical, untranslated segment that repeats itself in a document.
Review	The process of checking a translation in terms of conformance with the source text.
RTF	Abbreviation for **R**ich **T**ext **F**ormat. A cross-platform document file format.
SDL Trados Studio	A proprietary CAT Tool from SDL (http://www.sdl.com/cxc/language/translation-productivity/trados-studio/).
SDLPPX	SDL Trados Studio Project Package.
SDLRPX	SDL Trados Studio Return Package.
SDLTM	SDL Trados Studio TM.
SDLX	A proprietary, defunct CAT Tool from SDL.
SDLXLIFF	SDL Trados Studio bilingual file format.
Segment	(a.k.a. TU, Translation Unit) - A sentence or phrase that's defined by an ending punctuation mark.
Single Language Vendor	(a.k.a. SLV) - A company that provides single-language services, such as translation, localization, interpretation etc.

Term	Description
SLV	Abbreviation for **S**ingle **L**anguage **V**endor. A company that provides single-language services, such as translation, localization, interpretation etc.
SOB	Abbreviation for **S**tart **O**f **B**usiness. Indicates a specific time-frame that coincides with business opening hours.
Source File	A file that contains the original text for translation in its original form.
Source Language	Original language of the text to be translated.
SRX	Abbreviation for **S**egmentation **R**ules e**X**change. SRX provides a common way to describe how to segment text for translation and other language-related processes.
Star Transit	A proprietary CAT Tool from STAR Technology Solutions (http://www.star-ts.com).
Start Of Business	(a.k.a. SOB) - Indicates a specific time-frame that coincides with business opening hours.
Strings	Usually refers to extracted software text.
Style Guide	A document describing an official way of writing or translating material by using specific style, grammar, numeric formats etc.
Tag	Special blocks of code that precede and/or follow text that include style information or descriptors pertaining to that text.
TagEditor	A proprietary tag Editor part of SDL Trados Workbench CAT Tool.
Target File	(a.k.a. Clean File) - A file that contains the translated text in the source file's original form.
Target Language	The language in which the text will be translated.
TAT	Abbreviation for **T**urn **A**round **T**ime.
TBD	Abbreviation for **T**o **B**e **D**etermined.

Term	Description
TBX	Abbreviation for TermBase eXchange. An XML standard for exchanging Term-Bases.
TEP	Abbreviation for Translation Editing Proof-reading.
Term Extraction	The process of extracting terminology from source files using specialized software.
TermBase	Abbreviation for Terminology DataBase. A multi-lingual terminology database with terms and their definitions.
Terminology Database	(a.k.a. TermBase) - A multi-lingual terminology database with terms and their definitions.
TM	Abbreviation for Translation Memory. A database that retains all translations that are created during the translation process.
TMS	Abbreviation for Translation Management System. A program or platform that manages the full translation cycle or translation projects (file preparation, leveraging, task assigning, QA, delivery, invoicing etc.).
TMX	Abbreviation for Translation Memory eXchange. An XML standard for exchanging TMs.
Trados Workbench	A proprietary, defunct CAT Tool from SDL.
Transcreation	The process of adapting content from one language to another, while maintaining intent, style, tone and context.
Transcription	The process of transferring audio material (i.e., dialogues) into written form.
Translation Kit	A set of material which usually includes: source files, translation instructions, TM, TermBase, glossary etc.

Term	Description
Translation Management System	(a.k.a. TMS) - A program or platform that manages the full translation cycle or translation projects (file preparation, leveraging, task assigning, QA, delivery, invoicing etc.).
Translation Memory	(a.k.a. TM) - A database that retains all translations that are created during the translation process.
Translation Unit	(a.k.a. TU, Segment) - A sentence or phrase that's defined by a an ending punctuation mark.
Transliteration	The process of converting text from one language to another using the corresponding character set of the target language.
TTX	Trados TagEditor bilingual file format.
TU	(a.k.a. Segment) - Abbreviation for Translation Unit. A sentence or phrase that's defined by an ending punctuation mark.
TXML	Wordfast bilingual file format.
Unclean File	(a.k.a. Bilingual File) - A file that contains both the source text and the target translation. Usually refers to CAT Tool files.
Vendor Manager	The person responsible for finding, assessing and hiring freelancers.
VM	Abbreviation for Vendor Manager. The person responsible for finding, assessing and hiring freelancers.
Weighted Word Count	A single word count value representing a project's actual work volume, calculated by using the values from a TM Match Model and the TM log.
Word Count	Total number of words in a text.
Word Rate	(a.k.a. PPW) - The cost of a service based on a per word charge.
Wordfast	A proprietary CAT Tool from Wordfast (http://www.wordfast.com).

Term	Description
WWC	Abbreviation for **W**eighted **W**ord **C**ount. A single word count value representing a project's actual work volume, calculated by using the values from a TM Match Model and the TM log.
XLIFF	Abbreviation for **XML** Localisation Interchange **F**ile Format. An XML standard for exchanging bilingual files.
XLS	Microsoft Excel file format.
XLSX	Microsoft Excel file format.
XML	Abbreviation for E**X**tensible **M**arkup Language. A markup language that defines a set of rules for encoding documents in a format which is both human-readable and machine-readable.

Appendix 2: ISO Language Codes

Language Name	2-Letter Code (ISO 639-1)	3-Letter Code (ISO 639-2/T)
Abkhaz	AB	ABK
Afar	AA	AAR
Afrikaans	AF	AFR
Akan	AK	AKA
Albanian	SQ	SQI
Amharic	AM	AMH
Arabic	AR	ARA
Aragonese	AN	ARG
Armenian	HY	HYE
Assamese	AS	ASM
Avaric	AV	AVA
Avestan	AE	AVE
Aymara	AY	AYM
Azerbaijani	AZ	AZE
Bambara	BM	BAM
Bashkir	BA	BAK
Basque	EU	EUS
Belarusian	BE	BEL
Bengali, Bangla	BN	BEN
Bihari	BH	BIH
Bislama	BI	BIS
Bosnian	BS	BOS
Breton	BR	BRE
Bulgarian	BG	BUL
Burmese	MY	MYA
Catalan	CA	CAT
Chamorro	CH	CHA
Chechen	CE	CHE
Chichewa, Chewa, Nyanja	NY	NYA
Chinese	ZH	ZHO
Chuvash	CV	CHV

Language Name	2-Letter Code (ISO 639-1)	3-Letter Code (ISO 639-2/T)
Cornish	KW	COR
Corsican	CO	COS
Cree	CR	CRE
Croatian	HR	HRV
Czech	CS	CES
Danish	DA	DAN
Divehi, Dhivehi, Maldivian	DV	DIV
Dutch	NL	NLD
Dzongkha	DZ	DZO
English	EN	ENG
Esperanto	EO	EPO
Estonian	ET	EST
Ewe	EE	EWE
Faroese	FO	FAO
Fijian	FJ	FIJ
Finnish	FI	FIN
French	FR	FRA
Fula, Fulah, Pulaar, Pular	FF	FUL
Galician	GL	GLG
Georgian	KA	KAT
German	DE	DEU
Greek (modern)	EL	ELL
Guaraní	GN	GRN
Gujarati	GU	GUJ
Haitian, Haitian Creole	HT	HAT
Hausa	HA	HAU
Hebrew (modern)	HE	HEB
Herero	HZ	HER
Hindi	HI	HIN
Hiri Motu	HO	HMO
Hungarian	HU	HUN
Interlingua	IA	INA
Indonesian	ID	IND
Interlingue	IE	ILE
Irish	GA	GLE
Igbo	IG	IBO
Inupiaq	IK	IPK
Ido	IO	IDO

Language Name	2-Letter Code (ISO 639-1)	3-Letter Code (ISO 639-2/T)
Icelandic	IS	ISL
Italian	IT	ITA
Inuktitut	IU	IKU
Japanese	JA	JPN
Javanese	JV	JAV
Kalaallisut, Greenlandic	KL	KAL
Kannada	KN	KAN
Kanuri	KR	KAU
Kashmiri	KS	KAS
Kazakh	KK	KAZ
Khmer	KM	KHM
Kikuyu, Gikuyu	KI	KIK
Kinyarwanda	RW	KIN
Kyrgyz	KY	KIR
Komi	KV	KOM
Kongo	KG	KON
Korean	KO	KOR
Kurdish	KU	KUR
Kwanyama, Kuanyama	KJ	KUA
Latin	LA	LAT
Luxembourgish, Letzeburgesch	LB	LTZ
Ganda	LG	LUG
Limburgish, Limburgan, Limburger	LI	LIM
Lingala	LN	LIN
Lao	LO	LAO
Lithuanian	LT	LIT
Luba-Katanga	LU	LUB
Latvian	LV	LAV
Manx	GV	GLV
Macedonian	MK	MKD
Malagasy	MG	MLG
Malay	MS	MSA
Malayalam	ML	MAL
Maltese	MT	MLT
Māori	MI	MRI
Marathi (Marāṭhī)	MR	MAR
Marshallese	MH	MAH

Language Name	2-Letter Code (ISO 639-1)	3-Letter Code (ISO 639-2/T)
Mongolian	MN	MON
Nauru	NA	NAU
Navajo, Navaho	NV	NAV
Northern Ndebele	ND	NDE
Nepali	NE	NEP
Ndonga	NG	NDO
Norwegian Bokmål	NB	NOB
Norwegian Nynorsk	NN	NNO
Norwegian	NO	NOR
Nuosu	II	III
Southern Ndebele	NR	NBL
Occitan	OC	OCI
Ojibwe, Ojibwa	OJ	OJI
Oromo	OM	ORM
Oriya	OR	ORI
Ossetian, Ossetic	OS	OSS
Panjabi, Punjabi	PA	PAN
Pāli	PI	PLI
Persian (Farsi)	FA	FAS
Polish	PL	POL
Pashto, Pushto	PS	PUS
Portuguese	PT	POR
Quechua	QU	QUE
Romansh	RM	ROH
Kirundi	RN	RUN
Romanian	RO	RON
Russian	RU	RUS
Sanskrit (Saṁskṛta)	SA	SAN
Sardinian	SC	SRD
Sindhi	SD	SND
Northern Sami	SE	SME
Samoan	SM	SMO
Sango	SG	SAG
Serbian	SR	SRP
Scottish Gaelic, Gaelic	GD	GLA
Shona	SN	SNA
Sinhala, Sinhalese	SI	SIN
Slovak	SK	SLK
Slovene	SL	SLV

Language Name	2-Letter Code (ISO 639-1)	3-Letter Code (ISO 639-2/T)
Somali	SO	SOM
Southern Sotho	ST	SOT
Spanish	ES	SPA
Sundanese	SU	SUN
Swahili	SW	SWA
Swati	SS	SSW
Swedish	SV	SWE
Tamil	TA	TAM
Telugu	TE	TEL
Tajik	TG	TGK
Thai	TH	THA
Tigrinya	TI	TIR
Tibetan Standard, Tibetan, Central	BO	BOD
Turkmen	TK	TUK
Tagalog	TL	TGL
Tswana	TN	TSN
Tonga (Tonga Islands)	TO	TON
Turkish	TR	TUR
Tsonga	TS	TSO
Tatar	TT	TAT
Twi	TW	TWI
Tahitian	TY	TAH
Uyghur	UG	UIG
Ukrainian	UK	UKR
Urdu	UR	URD
Uzbek	UZ	UZB
Venda	VE	VEN
Vietnamese	VI	VIE
Volapük	VO	VOL
Walloon	WA	WLN
Welsh	CY	CYM
Wolof	WO	WOL
Western Frisian	FY	FRY
Xhosa	XH	XHO
Yiddish	YI	YID
Yoruba	YO	YOR
Zhuang, Chuang	ZA	ZHA
Zulu	ZU	ZUL

Appendix 3: List of Translation Companies

Company Name	Application Method (Email or Web Form)
1-Stop Translation USA, LLC	info@1stopasia.com
101Translations	http://www.101translations.com/content/contact-us/5
AAC Global	http://www.aacglobal.com/careers/recruitment-form/
Able Translations Ltd.	http://www.abletranslations.com/?pager=joinTeam
ACADEMICWORD	http://www.academicword.com/emp.asp
Acclaro Inc.	http://acclaro.applicantstack.com/x/openings
Accredited Language Services	https://www.alsintl.com/job-opportunities/language-specialists/
Accurapid	http://www.accurapid.com/contact/translator-application/
ADH Avrasya Translation	http://www.avrasyatranslation.com/en/?page_id=7721
AETI	http://www.eurotrad.org/et/eng/tl/
Agostini & Associati Srl	http://www.agostiniassociati.it/qvf_eng.php
aiaTranslations LLC	https://creator.zoho.com/marhodesnaughton/aiatranslations/form-perma/Freelancer_Application
Alkemist	zaposlitev@alkemist.si
All Languages Ltd.	http://outside.alllanguages.com/application.asp
Améredia Inc.	work@ameredia.com
ASET International Services LLC	comlanguage@experis.com
ASIST Translation Services, Inc.	info@asisttranslations.com
Barbier International	http://www.barbierintl.com/careers/

Company Name	Application Method (Email or Web Form)
BeTranslated	http://www.betranslated.com/freelance-translators-database.html
Broad Solutions, LLC.	jobs@BroadSolutionsGroup.com
Capita Translation and Interpreting	http://www.capitatranslationinterpreting.com/work-us/
CET Central European Translations	http://www.cet-translations.com/translator-registration/
CETRA, Inc.	http://www.cetra.com/careers/
Cillero & de Motta	http://www.cillerodemotta.com/en/cv2.asp
CLI Solutions	recruiting.agent@theatarigroup.com
Codex Global Limited	vendormanagement@codexglobal.net
Comms Multilingual	http://www.commsmultilingual.com/contact-us/providers/
Communicaid Inc.	http://www.communicaidinc.com/contact/employment.php
Continental Interpreting Services Inc.	http://www.cis-inc.com/linguists/submit-resume/
Corporate Translations	http://www.corptransinc.com/Translator-Application.aspx
Cosmiceurope Limited	info@cosmiceurope.com
CP Language Institute	apply@cpli.com
CPW Group	http://www.cpw-group.com/en/careers.htm
e2f	https://e2f.com/about-us/employment/freelancers/
ElaN Languages	http://www.elanlanguages.com/en/join-our-team/translators
euroscript	http://www.euroscript.com/cs/Satellite?c=Page&childpagename=Euroscript%2FESCLayout&cid=1349859995844&pagename=ESCWrapperForm
EVS Translations	http://www.evs-translations.com/career/freelance/
ForeignExchange Translations	vm@fxtrans.com
Gemino GmbH	https://gemino.de/en/oap/

Company Name	Application Method (Email or Web Form)
Get It	vendors@getit.eu
Global Language Solutions	http://www.globallanguages.com/en/contactus/vendor_freelance.php
Global Lingo Ltd.	WorkWithUs@global-lingo.com
GlobalVision International	infonow@globalvis.com
GlobeSoft	Hr@globe-soft.net
Honyaku Center Inc.	http://www.honyakuctren.com/freelance_b.html
idealTrans	http://www.idealtrans.net/JoinUs.aspx
Intercombase Translation Company	info@intercombase.com
JONCKERS	translators@jonckers.com
K International	http://www.k-international.com/about-us/join-the-team/
kalimera	https://aplicatie.kalimera.ro/vendors/#/sign-up
KERN Global Language Services	http://www.e-kern.com/us/company/vacancies/freelancers.html
Kosmos Srl	http://www.kosmostranslations.co.uk/work-with-us/enter-your-cv/
Laird Assessors	http://www.laird-assessors.com/about/careers-with-us/
Language Scientific, Inc.	cv@languagescientific.com
Language Services Associates	https://lsaweb.com/careers/linguists/
LanguageWorks	resources@languageworks.com
Lingo24	http://www.lingo24.com/new_translators.html
Lingo365	http://www.lingo365.com/translation-login
Linguava Interpreters	careers@linguava.com
Linguistic Systems, Inc.	https://sts.linguist.com/LinguistPortal/
Lionbridge	https://partners.lionbridge.com/WorkWithUs/Introduction.aspx

Company Name	Application Method (Email or Web Form)
Local Concept	hr@localconcept.com
LocaTran Translations Ltd.	http://www.locatran.com/eng/carees.asp
LUZ, Inc.	translation.partners@luz.com
MAart Sp. z o.o.	http://www.maart.com/en/join-us.html
MasterWord	http://www.masterword.com/careers/mws-careers-in-freelance/
MEJ Personal Business Services Inc.	http://www.mejpbs.com/newemployees.php
Morningside Translations, Inc.	tv@morningtrans.com
Nouveau Language	hr@nouveau.fi
One Global	https://oneglobal.s.xtrf.eu/partners/faces/noLogin/provider/identificationData.seam?action=create&conversationId=14080
Planet Lingua	rrhh@planetlingua.com
Prestige Network	http://www.prestigenetwork.com/Home/Contact/Careers/Freelance-Translator.aspx
ProTranslating	http://www.protranslating.com/careers/freelance
Scribendi Inc.	http://www.scribendi.com/apply
SimulTrans LLC	http://www.simultrans.com/careers
SPĚVÁČEK Language Services Group	http://www.spevacek.info/en/career/translator/
Strategic Agenda	recruitment@strategicagenda.com
Techworld Language Solutions	http://techworldinc.com/about/careers/
TEXTKING	https://www.textking.com/partner/start
Textronics Communications Ltd.	info@textronics.com
The Geo Group	vendormanager@thegeogroup.com
The Marketing Analysts	http://www.themarketinganalysts.com/en/contacts/
thebigword Group Plc.	https://gms.thebigword.com/linguist/signup

Company Name	Application Method (Email or Web Form)
Tilde	darbs@tilde.lv
tolingo GmbH	https://www.tolingo.com/sites/en/vendors
TransGlocal, LLC	https://www.transglocal.org/Contact_Us.php
TRANSLAB Hellas	http://www.translab.gr/new_supplier.php?lang=en
Translate 24/7	careers@translate24-7.com
Translated	https://www.translated.net/top/
TranslateMedia	http://www.translatemedia.com/us/jobs/
Translation Empire	http://www.translation-empire.com/join-us-2/translation-empire/register-as-a-translator/
Translation Services USA	https://www.translation-services-usa.com/itranslate/
Translatum Oy	recruit@translatum.fi
TRAVOD	http://www.travod.com/Career.html
Trusted Translations, Inc.	http://www.trustedtranslations.net/translator-jobs/
Ubiqus	http://www.ubiqus.com/contact-us/jobs/application/
Universe Translation Inc.	http://www.universe.us/translator/index.cfm?action=register
Verbatim Solutions	translators@verbatimsolutions.com
VIA	careers@viadelivers.com
Vinclu	http://www.vinclu.com/en/about/recruitment/
Wordbank	freelance_recruitment@wordbank.com
Yamagata Europe	https://suppliersnet.yamagata-europe.com/RegistrationForm/RegistrationGeneralInfo.aspx
ZELENKA	http://portal.zelenka.cz/interpreter/registration/en-gb

Made in the USA
Lexington, KY
31 October 2018